VALUE AND VIRTUE IN A GODLESS UNIVERSE

Suppose there is no God. Would the implication be that human life is meaningless, that the notions of right and wrong, virtue and vice, good and evil
have no place, and that there are no moral obligations – hence people can
do whatever they want? Erik J. Wielenberg believes this view to be utterly
mistaken and in this book he explains why. He argues that even if God does
not exist, human life can have meaning, we do have moral obligations, and
virtue is possible. Naturally, the author sees virtue in a Godless universe as
significantly different from virtue in a Christian universe, and he develops
naturalistic accounts of humility, charity, and hope. The moral landscape
in a Godless universe is different from the moral landscape in a Christian
universe, but it does indeed exist. *Value and Virtue in a Godless Universe* is a
tour of some of the central landmarks of this underexplored territory.

Erik J. Wielenberg is Assistant Professor of Philosophy at DePauw Univer-
sity. He has written articles in such journals as *Religious Studies, Faith and
Philosophy, Pacific Philosophical Quarterly, Synthese*, and *Oxford Studies in Ancient
Philosophy*.

VALUE AND VIRTUE IN A GODLESS UNIVERSE

ERIK J. WIELENBERG

DePauw University

CAMBRIDGE
UNIVERSITY PRESS

CAMBRIDGE UNIVERSITY PRESS
Cambridge, New York, Melbourne, Madrid, Cape Town, Singapore, São Paulo

Cambridge University Press
40 West 20th Street, New York, NY 10011-4211, USA

www.cambridge.org
Information on this title: www.cambridge.org/9780521845656

First published 2005
Reprinted 2005

Printed in the United States of America

A catalog record for this publication is available from the British Library.

Library of Congress Cataloging in Publication Data
Wielenberg, Erik J. (Erik Joseph), 1972–
Value and virtue in a godless universe / Erik J. Wielenberg.
　　p.　cm.
Includes bibliographical references and index.
ISBN 0-521-84565-3 – ISBN 0-521-60784-1 (pbk.)
1. Religion and ethics.　2. Atheism.　3. Values.　I. Title.
BJ47.W54　2005
170 – dc22　　　2004018633

ISBN-13　978-0-521-84565-6 hardback
ISBN-10　0-521-84565-3 hardback

ISBN-13　978-0-521-60784-1 paperback
ISBN-10　0-521-60784-1 paperback

For Margaret,
a group number one person

"Many a man has borne himself proudly on the scaffold; surely the same pride should teach us to think truly about man's place in the world."

– Bertrand Russell, *What I Believe* (1925)

CONTENTS

Contents

ACKNOWLEDGMENTS

No accomplishment, no matter how modest, is entirely the result of a single person's efforts. This modest book is no exception. In writing this book, I have benefited from many happy turns of chance and from the presence and assistance of a variety of persons and institutions. I attempt to acknowledge them here and ask the forgiveness of any I may have omitted.

Several people read parts of the various earlier versions of the manuscript, and many of these people gave helpful comments and advice. I would like to thank Noah Lemos, Keith Nightenhelser, William Placher, Aaron Wielenberg, Margaret Dewey Wielenberg, and the Cambridge University Press editors and readers for their assistance. I would also like to thank Scott Senn for his assistance in the translation of various works written in ancient Greek, including the epigraph for Chapter 2.

I am grateful to my colleagues in the philosophy department and the students who have taken my courses at DePauw University. The former provided a congenial and supportive atmosphere and the opportunity to develop new courses, which in turn allowed me to develop many of the ideas found in this book. The latter provided feedback concerning those ideas and, in some cases, the motivation to explore certain strands of thought further. I am particularly grateful to the first-year students who took my seminar on the philosophical works of C. S. Lewis in the fall of 2002 and the students in my upper-level courses on moral character and the philosophy of religion.

John Pardee, my high school English teacher, once told the immature and erratic student I was in high school that "you can only

Acknowledgments

get by on potential for so long." Though a few years passed before
these words began to take effect, John Pardee was the first of several
persons who crucially influenced my academic career. John Dreher,
Ned Markosian, and Tim Spurgin introduced me to philosophy at
Lawrence University, and Tom Ryckman saw that the immature and
still fairly erratic student I was in college might have the potential
to study philosophy at the graduate level. I did my graduate work
at the University of Massachusetts–Amherst, where I was lucky to
fall under the influence of several excellent teachers, none more so
than my dissertation director, Fred Feldman, under whose guidance
and penetrating criticism I finally managed to produce work in philosophy that I would not be embarrassed by today. While finishing
my dissertation, I spent a year as a graduate student Fellow at the
Center for Philosophy of Religion at the University of Notre Dame,
where I benefited tremendously from my interaction with the other
members of the Center, particularly Alvin Plantinga and Tom Flint.

Tradition dictates that the most important acknowledgments come
last, and I will follow tradition in this case. This book surely would
not exist were it not for the contributions of two people in particular.
The first is my mother, Peggy Wielenberg, whom I thank for her
unwavering support, her belief in the value of education, and what
surely must have been her superhuman restraint in allowing me to
find my own path. The second is my wife, Margaret, whom I thank
for her continuous love, the emotional framework that made the
writing of this book possible, and her faith that I really was writing a
book as she went off to work each day during the summer of 2003.

I am confident that the majority of the people I have listed here
would disagree with much of what I have to say in the book. Some
of them, moreover, would find parts of the book to be at odds with
deeply held beliefs. I hope that they will take the book in the spirit
of inquiry in which it was intended. Of course the responsibility for
the errors that the book undoubtedly contains is mine alone.

Plainfield, Indiana
March 2004

x

INTRODUCTION

Director M. Night Shyamalan's (2002) film *Signs* is remarkable in that it is simultaneously a story about an attempted invasion of the earth by extraterrestrials and an examination of religious faith. The main character is Graham Hess, a modern-day Job who has lost his faith as a result of his wife's tragic death. At one point in the film, Graham and his brother Merrill are watching news reports about the activity of alien ships. Graham makes the following speech:

> People break down into two groups when they experience something lucky. Group number one sees it as more than luck, more than coincidence. They see it as a sign, evidence, that there is someone up there, watching out for them. Group number two sees it as just pure luck. Just a happy turn of chance. I'm sure the people in group number two are looking at those fourteen lights in a very suspicious way. For them, the situation is fifty-fifty. Could be bad, could be good. But deep down, they feel that whatever happens, they're on their own. And that fills them with fear. Yeah, there are those people. But there's a whole lot of people in group number one. When they see those fourteen lights, they're looking at a miracle. And deep down, they feel that whatever's going to happen, there will be someone there to help them. And that fills them with hope. See, what you have to ask yourself is, what kind of person are you? Are you the kind that sees signs, sees miracles? Or do you believe that people just get lucky?[1]

Graham's remarks do an excellent job of characterizing the two sides of an ancient debate. In the contemporary Western philosophical scene, the two parties to this debate are typically theists on the one hand and atheists or naturalists on the other.

1

The central project of this book is an examination of the ethical implications of *naturalism*. It is essential, therefore, that I offer some account of what I mean by that term. The central component of naturalism is the claim that no supernatural entities exist, nor have such entities existed in the past, nor will they in the future. I could spill a lot of ink trying to develop philosophically precise analyses of the concepts of *natural* and *supernatural*. Fortunately, I do not believe this is necessary for my purposes. I think our intuitive grasp of the sorts of entities that might reasonably be characterized as supernatural is sufficiently clear and includes the God of each of the three major monotheistic religions (Judaism, Christianity, and Islam) as well as nonphysical souls of the sort posited by Descartes and others. Naturalism entails that none of these things exists. As I understand it, naturalism also implies that death marks the permanent end of conscious experience for the one who dies: There is no afterlife or reincarnation in a naturalistic universe.

Naturalism in my sense does not, however, include certain stronger theses that are sometimes associated with the term. It does not, for instance, include the claim that all facts are scientific facts, or that all truths can be stated in the language of science. Specifically, naturalism leaves open the possibility that there are ethical facts that are not reducible to physical or scientific facts. Some versions of materialism entail that ethical facts, if there are any, are in this way reducible. Though such versions of materialism would not be inconsistant with naturalism, in my view they are false. My version of naturalism also does not imply that there is no *a priori* knowledge. The brand of naturalism I hold is primarily an *ontological* thesis. In a naturalistic universe, there is no God, no afterlife, and no immortal soul.

On the positive side, naturalism includes a story about how human beings came into existence. The basic elements of the story are described by the contemporary Christian philosopher Alvin Plantinga (2000) as follows:

> We human beings arrived on the scene after...billions of years of organic evolution. In the beginning, there was just inorganic matter;

somehow, and by way of processes of which we currently have no grasp, life, despite its enormous and daunting complexity at even the simplest level, arose from nonliving matter, and arose just by way of the regularities studied in physics and chemistry. Once life arose, random genetic mutation and natural selection, those great twin engines of evolution, swung into action. These genetic mutations are multiply random: they weren't intended by anyone, of course, but also were not directed by any sort of natural teleology. . . . Occasionally, some of them yield an adaptive advantage; their possessors come to predominate in the populations, and they are passed on to the next and subsequent generations. In this way, all the enormous variety of flora and fauna we behold came into being. Including ourselves. . . . [2]

Although Plantinga's skepticism about the truth of this story peeks through in his account of it, the description is accurate. According to naturalism, then, human beings came into existence through a combination of necessity and chance. What is notably absent in our naturalistic origin is the operation of intelligent design. According to my version of naturalism, intelligent design played no role in the formation of the natural universe. I will not affix any particular cosmological theory to naturalism. For our purposes here, it is sufficient to note that naturalism denies that the universe or anything in it was created by God, gods, or any other supernatural being.

In this book I will not argue for the truth of naturalism. My project instead will be a conditional one: Let us suppose that naturalism is true. What are the ethical implications of such a view? Does it imply, for instance, that human life has no meaning, or that nothing is right or wrong? Does it imply that we should be entirely selfish, and that it is irrational or pointless to try to help our fellow humans? Is there such a thing as virtue in a naturalistic universe, and if so, what is it? These are the sorts of questions I will address, in the course of which I will discuss the arguments and views of certain Christian writers. I will sometimes draw attention to areas of contrast or similarity between my naturalistic view and the Christian view. I focus on Christianity primarily because it is the religious outlook with which I am most familiar. This book is, in part, a response to arguments made by certain Christian philosophers who sometimes seek to refute naturalism by claiming that it has all sorts of nasty

ethical implications. Naturalism has been variously accused of implying nihilism, relativism, hedonism, or egoism. I will rebut these
arguments.

Before turning to the main task of the book, however, I would
like to provide a brief, two-part account of why I am not a Christian.
The first part is a very brief psychological explanation of why I do not
accept the truth of Christianity. The second part is a brief defense of
the claim that it is reasonable for me to persist in my nonacceptance.

Although I was raised in the Lutheran tradition and confirmed
into the Lutheran church, the doctrines never really took. I was
always at least a bit skeptical of the Christian version of the origin
of the universe and of humans, and of its supernatural claims about
Jesus. Large parts of the story just sounded made up to me. When I
got a bit older I studied the mythologies of various cultures in school,
and it seemed increasingly clear to me that Christianity was simply a
myth that was widely accepted in my own culture. The notion that
it was actually true did not seem plausible.[3]

I need also to defend the claim that it is reasonable for me to
continue to withhold belief in the truth of Christianity. There are,
broadly speaking, two related types of argument that might make
it irrational for me to persist in my rejection of Christianity.[4] First,
there are the various philosophical attempts to prove the existence of
God. A proper discussion of these arguments is a huge task and is well
beyond the scope of the present work. All I can do here is record my
conviction that all such arguments are unsuccessful. None of them
makes a convincing case for the existence of an omnipotent, omniscient, morally perfect creator. Indeed, many of these arguments,
even if entirely successful, would still fail to establish the existence of
such a being. This is because many of these philosophical arguments
fail to provide any reason at all for believing that an omnipotent, omniscient creator of the universe also would be morally perfect. The
two exceptions of which I am aware are the ontological argument
and some types of moral argument. But these exceptions, I think,
are defective for other reasons.

One venerable type of philosophical argument is the so-called design argument.[5] Design arguments generally start with an empirical

observation about the natural universe that allegedly indicates the operation of intelligent design at work in the universe. Although some versions of the design argument are undermined by evolutionary theory, not all are, and this kind of argument remains, in my view, the most interesting of the theistic arguments for God's existence. The contemporary "fine-tuning" argument is, for instance, worthy of serious attention.[6] But design arguments, like so many others, give us no reason at all to think that the intelligent designer of the universe would be morally perfect. Indeed, the arguments tell us nothing at all about the moral characteristics of the designer. In connection with this point we should notice the differences between the following three propositions:

1. Intelligent design played some role in the formation of the natural universe.
2. The universe was created by an omnipotent, omniscient, morally perfect being.
3. The Christian God exists, and the various Christian claims about history and about Jesus are true.

The gaps between propositions (1) and (2) and between (2) and (3) are large. One can certainly accept (1) without accepting (2). In his classic work *Dialogues Concerning Natural Religion*, the great atheistic eighteenth-century Scottish philosopher David Hume (1998a) has the character Philo reach the following conclusion on the basis of his observation of the mixture of good and evil in the universe:

> There may *four* hypotheses be framed concerning the first causes of the universe: *that* they are endowed with perfect goodness; *that* they have perfect malice; *that* they are opposite and have both goodness and malice; *that* they have neither goodness nor malice. Mixed phenomena can never prove the two former unmixed principles; and the uniformity and steadiness of general laws seem to oppose the third. The fourth, therefore, seems by far the most probable.[7]

Hume hits the nail right on the head here. It is hard to see how observation of the distribution of good and evil in the universe could suggest the presence of a morally perfect creator. A morally indifferent creator or source seems to be the most probable hypothesis based on the available empirical evidence about how good and evil are distributed. Perhaps this evidence could be outweighed by sufficiently compelling grounds for believing in a morally perfect creator. But I know of no such grounds. One can also accept proposition (2) without accepting (3). Indeed, proposition (2) is common to Judaism, Christianity, and Islam. Now, the philosophical arguments I have alluded to, even if successful, would establish *at most* proposition (2), and it is still a long way from there to proposition (3). Even if philosophy could establish proposition (2), something more would be needed to take us to Christianity. This is where the second kind of argument enters the picture.

The second kind of argument is a historical argument for the truth of the Christian claims about Jesus. This kind of argument is based on various bits of empirical evidence, including, for example, the testimony of the gospel writers and others, as well as archaeological evidence. This argument involves an *inference to the best explanation*. The suggestion is that the best explanation for the various bits of relevant evidence is that Jesus really did perform various miracles, He really did rise from the dead, and, most importantly, He really was the son of God. This kind of argument recently has been defended by Lee Strobel (1998) in his popular book *The Case for Christ*.

Hume (1998b) discusses this kind of argument in his essay "Of Miracles." He lays down the maxim that "no testimony is sufficient to establish a miracle unless the testimony be of such a kind that its falsehood would be more miraculous than the fact which it endeavors to establish."[8] Hume's maxim is concerned exclusively with testimony, but his basic point can be extended to all kinds of historical evidence. I think Hume is directing us to consider the relative probabilities of two scenarios. He is suggesting that we should ask ourselves, in the case of any alleged miracle, whether it is more likely that a miracle actually occurred or that the evidence for the miracle has a purely natural explanation. Hume's suggestion is that, at least when the evidence in question consists of testimony of some kind, the latter possibility is *always* more probable than the former. He concludes that "no human testimony can have such force as to prove a miracle, and make it a just foundation for any...system of religion."[9]

Hume's remarks suggest the following position: To evaluate the adequacy of historical arguments for the truth of various Christian claims about Jesus, we must compare the probabilities of two scenarios. The first is that the Christian claims are true. The second is that there is some purely natural explanation for the various bits of relevant historical evidence. What I will call "the Humean Position" is that in every case the second scenario is the more likely one, and hence no historical argument for the truth of Christianity can succeed.[10]

The twentieth-century Christian apologist C. S. Lewis's (2001c) book *Miracles* is a response to Hume's essay. The opening chapter of that book contains the following passage:

> Many people think that one can decide whether a miracle occurred in the past by examining the evidence 'according to the ordinary rules of historical inquiry'. But the ordinary rules cannot be worked until we have decided whether miracles are probable, and if so, how probable they are. For if they are impossible, then no amount of historical evidence will convince us. If they are possible but immensely improbable, then only mathematically demonstrative evidence will convince us: and since history never provides that degree of evidence for any event, history can never convince us that a miracle occurred. If, on the other hand, miracles are not intrinsically improbable, then the existing evidence will be sufficient to convince us that quite a number of miracles have occurred. *The result of our historical enquiries thus depends on the philosophical views which we have been holding before we even began to look at the evidence. This philosophical question must therefore come first.*[11]

Lewis notes that the historical argument depends on a "philosophical question," which is, how likely is it that miracles occur in our universe? Hume and Lewis agree, then, that whether the historical argument can succeed depends on how likely it is that miracles occur in our universe. The Humean Position is that miracles are extremely unlikely – so unlikely, in fact, that for any alleged historical miracle, it is more likely that the relevant evidence has a purely natural explanation than that the miracle actually occurred. And I think that position is correct. It is important to see that I am not arguing that no miracles have ever occurred; rather, I am arguing that, even if such miracles have occurred, it is not rational for us to infer that they have occurred based on historical evidence. Historical evidence can *never* be powerful enough to counterbalance the extreme improbability of such events. Moreover, in the particular case of Christianity, both the quantity and the quality of the available historical evidence are a matter of debate. For instance, in her book *A History of God*, Karen Armstrong (1993) writes:

> We know very little about Jesus. The first full-length account of his life was St. Mark's Gospel, which was not written until about the year 70, some forty years after his death. By that time, historical facts had been overlaid with mythical elements which expressed the meaning Jesus had acquired for his followers. It is this meaning that St. Mark primarily conveys rather than a reliable straightforward portrayal.[12]

Still, the fundamental problem with the historical argument is a philosophical one. The issue of the quality of the historical evidence for the truth of Christianity is something of a red herring. *No* evidence of this sort could make it rational to infer that the alleged miracles actually took place.

The very dependence that both Hume and Lewis point to is acknowledged by contemporary Christian philosopher William Lane Craig in his interview with Lee Strobel as it appears in *The Case for Christ*. Strobel and Craig are discussing the issue of whether Jesus was really resurrected from the dead, when Strobel asks Craig about various alternative theories that have been proposed. This provokes the following crucial exchange in which Craig speaks first:

> "This, I think, is the issue," he said, leaning forward. "I think people who push these alternative theories would admit, 'Yes, our theories are implausible, but they're not as improbable as the idea that this spectacular miracle occurred.' *However, at this point, the matter is no longer a historical issue; instead it's a philosophical question about whether miracles are possible.*"
> "And what," I asked, "would you say to that?"
> "I would argue that the hypothesis that God raised Jesus from the dead is not at all improbable. In fact, based on the evidence, it's the best

explanation for what happened.... The hypothesis that God raised Jesus from the dead doesn't contradict science or any known facts of experience. *All it requires is the hypothesis that God exists, and I think there are good independent reasons for believing that he does.*"[13]

I, on the other hand, do not think that there are good independent reasons for believing that God (understood in the way specified by proposition [2]) exists. Hume, Lewis, and Craig all agree that the historical argument depends on the philosophical arguments; what they disagree about is the status of the philosophical arguments. Like so many debates, this one comes down to philosophy. Because I do not find the philosophical arguments convincing, I assign a very low probability to the occurrence of the alleged miracles and consequently find the historical arguments unconvincing. If there were a convincing argument for proposition (2), then perhaps sufficiently strong historical evidence could move us from (2) to (3). But without a good reason to accept (2), no amount of historical evidence can get us to (3).

What, it might be asked, is my naturalistic explanation of the various pieces of historical evidence for Christian claims about Jesus? If, for instance, Jesus wasn't really raised from the dead, what *did* happen? My answer is that I do not know, at least not in any precise way. The events in question took place roughly two thousand years ago and it may be the case that it is impossible to be certain exactly what happened based on the evidence available to us now. Hume wrote that "the knavery and folly of men are such common phenomena, that I should rather believe the most extraordinary events to arise from their concurrence, then admit of... a violation of the laws of nature."[14] When we add to this equation the propensity of humans to spread juicy gossip, the political and social situation at the time Jesus lived, and the message of hope offered by Jesus, we can begin to see how the Christian version of the life of Jesus might have become so widely believed. But I am afraid I cannot get much more specific than this.

Perhaps it will be objected that unless I can provide a sufficiently specific alternative explanation, it is irrational for me to reject the Christian explanation. But the principle underlying this objection – that a given explanation can be rejected rationally only if there is a sufficiently specific alternative explanation available – is false. The style of inference known as "the inference to the best explanation" would be labeled more accurately "the inference to the best *and sufficiently good* explanation." Some explanations are so bad that they can and should be rejected even if no detailed alternative explanation is available. And one way in which an explanation can be bad is by being extremely improbable. Reflection on some cases will reveal that this is so.

Tabloid magazines are filled with accounts of incredible events. For awhile, reported sightings of Elvis Presley abounded. Must we examine all the available evidence for such events and develop detailed alternative explanations before it is rational for us to reject the claim that the incredible event in question actually took place? Of course not. We do not need to interview the witnesses, inspect the physical evidence, and devise alternative scenarios to reject rationally the notion that Elvis really was spotted recently at a Blackjack table in Las Vegas. In a similar vein, I offer the following argument specifically for Christians. There are many religions in the world aside from Christianity. Many of these contain their own sacred texts and their own alleged prophets and miracles. Have you examined the historical evidence for such miracles and developed detailed alternative explanations of those miracles? If not, then you cannot consistently maintain that my failure to accept the historical argument for Christianity is irrational while simultaneously rejecting the miraculous claims of these other religions. In the words of Stephen Roberts, "[W]hen you understand why you dismiss all the other possible gods, you will understand why I dismiss yours."[15]

Moreover, ancient histories contain many accounts of supernatural occurrences. For instance, Plutarch's (1960) account of the life of Themistocles contains the following description of an event that allegedly took place during a naval battle between the Greeks and the Persians:

> At this point in the battle it is said that a great light suddenly shone out from Elusius and a loud cry seemed to fill the whole breadth of

the Thriasian plain down to the sea, as though an immense crowd were escorting the mystic Iacchus in procession. Then, from the place where the shouting was heard, a cloud seemed to rise slowly from the land, drift out to sea, and descend upon the triremes. Others believed that they saw phantoms and the shapes of armed men coming from Aegina with hands outstretched to protect the Greek ships. These, they believed, were the sons of Aecus, to whom they had offered prayers for help just before the battle.[16]

Now, I don't have the slightest notion of what actually happened here, and I suspect you do not either. Yet it hardly follows that it is irrational for us to reject the hypothesis that the phantom sons of Aecus answered the prayers for help. Similarly, it is perfectly rational for me to reject the Christian supernatural claims about Jesus without having a detailed alternative explanation. The historical arguments for Christianity depend on the philosophical arguments for the existence of God. Because I do not find the latter convincing, I reject the former. This, in brief, is why I still am not a Christian.[17]

The structure of the rest of the book is as follows. In the first chapter I critically examine three arguments for the claim that if God does not exist, then all human lives are meaningless. I suggest that all three arguments fail and that at least some human lives can be meaningful even if God does not exist. The second chapter includes a critical examination of a fourth argument for the claim that without God, all human lives are meaningless. This argument, if successful, would show that if God does not exist, there are no ethical facts at all. After refuting this argument, I consider a more modest suggestion that is sometimes called "Karamazov's Thesis" after some remarks by Alyosha Karamazov in Dostoevsky's novel *The Brothers Karamazov*. This is the claim that if God does not exist, then all actions are morally permissible. I argue that this more modest suggestion is false as well, and I outline what I take to be the truth about the relationship between God (if He exists) and ethical truth. This account implies that there are ethical truths even if, as I believe, God does not exist.

In the third chapter I consider the position that without God, while we may have certain moral obligations, we have no particular reason to care about what our obligations are. This position relates to the ancient question of why we should be moral. I outline one theistic response to this question based on the notion that there is a divine guarantee of perfect justice. I also discuss a few possible responses to the question that are consistent with naturalism. I endorse one of these, a Kantian answer, and argue that the question of why we should be moral can be answered even in a naturalistic universe. The chapter concludes with a critical examination of a few moral arguments for God's existence, including Kant's (1997) moral argument from the *Critique of Practical Reason*.

The fourth chapter focuses on virtuous character in a naturalistic universe. Specifically, I consider whether there is room for humility, charity, and hope in such a universe. I argue that there is, and say a bit about what form these virtues might take without God in the picture. Naturalistic versions of these three virtues would, of course, differ from Christian versions, and I examine some areas of contrast between naturalistic humility, charity, and hope, and their Christian counterparts. In latter sections of the chapter I examine our situation in the universe if naturalism is true, and consider what our attitude toward that situation should be. The chapter concludes with a discussion of the importance of the ancient Platonic quest for a reliable way of making people virtuous, and I propose one way that quest might be pursued in a naturalistic universe.

In the fifth and final chapter I consider the suggestion (which goes back at least as far as Plato) that we should try to inculcate acceptance of certain supernatural claims not because they are true but because widespread acceptance of such claims would have good consequences. I argue that the Old Testament contains certain elements that make any system of belief that includes them a poor candidate for promulgation on such grounds. The chapter and the book ends with a discussion of the question of whether naturalism is a creed we can live by. My answer, in brief, is that naturalism is a creed that some can live by and some cannot. However, whether it is a creed we can live by and whether it is true are two different issues. It may be that naturalism is a truth that many people cannot accept.

The overarching goal of the book is to say something interesting about what ethics might look like without God. In earlier chapters I am concerned primarily with showing that there can be ethical truths of various kinds even if God does not exist. In later chapters I am concerned primarily with exploring what some of these ethical truths might be. Another way of putting this is to say that earlier chapters are concerned with the *existence* of ethics without God, whereas later chapters are concerned with the *nature* of ethics without God.

ONE

GOD AND THE MEANING OF LIFE

1.1 THE MEANINGS OF LIFE

It is often maintained that if God does not exist then human life is meaningless. There are a number of ways one might interpret this claim, depending on how one understands what it is for a human life to have meaning. Under one interpretation, for a human life to have meaning is for it to have a purpose that is assigned by a supernatural being. When a life has meaning in this sense we can say that it has *supernatural meaning*. Socrates apparently believed that his life had supernatural meaning, and he speculated about what the purpose of his life might be during his famous trial:

> [I]f you put me to death, you will not easily find another who . . . clings to the state as a sort of gadfly to a horse that is well-bred and sluggish because of its size, so that it needs to be aroused. It seems to me that the god has attached me like that to the state, for I am constantly alighting upon you at every point to arouse, persuade, and reproach each of you all day long.[1]

According to the Christian tradition, the life of Jesus had supernatural meaning: Among its purposes was to atone for the sins of humanity. Indeed, according to some versions of Christianity, every human life shares a common purpose: to glorify God and enjoy Him forever.[2]

Under another interpretation, for a human life to have meaning is for it to bring goodness into the universe. When a life has meaning in this sense, the universe is better than it would have been had the life not been lived. We can say that a life of this sort has *external meaning*.

Again according to Christian tradition, the life of Jesus, in addition to having supernatural meaning, had external meaning. According to that tradition, a universe in which Jesus lived the life He did is far better than a universe in which no such life is ever lived.[3]

Under a third interpretation, for a human life to have meaning is for it to be good for the person who lives it and for it to include activity that is worthwhile. When a life has meaning in this sense, the individual is better off having lived than had that person never existed at all. Moreover, the life is one in which something worthwhile is accomplished. It is a life that has a point. It is the urge to live a life like this that is revealed in the expression "I want to *do* something with my life." We can say that a life of this sort has *internal meaning*. This concept may seem similar to external meaning, but the two are distinct. It is possible for a life to have internal meaning yet lack external meaning. Suppose a person engages in worthwhile activity that brings him pleasure and gives his life internal meaning. Suppose further that what gives his activity worth is that through it he accomplishes some meaningful goal. But suppose that if he had never lived, the same goal would have been accomplished by someone else who would have enjoyed accomplishing it just as much as he did. In this case, his life lacks external meaning because the universe would have been just as good if he had never lived. Yet his life has internal meaning. At least initially, it appears that it is also possible for a life to have external meaning but lack internal meaning. Such a life might be lived by someone who sacrifices his own happiness for the sake of others.

These, then, are three of the most natural understandings of what it is for a human life to have meaning. With these in hand, we are ready to consider the oft-made claim that without God, human life is meaningless.

1.2 FOUR ARGUMENTS THAT LIFE LACKS INTERNAL MEANING WITHOUT GOD

One way of understanding the claim that the nonexistence of God renders human life meaningless is as the thesis that if God does not exist, then no human life has internal meaning. A wide range of arguments might be offered in support of this thesis. The first of these is the *final outcome argument*. To get the flavor of this argument, consider the following remarks made by William Lane Craig (2004) in a talk called "The Absurdity of Life Without God" delivered at the Academy of Christian Apologetics:

> Scientists tell us that everything in the universe is growing farther and farther apart. As it does so, the universe grows colder and colder, and its energy is used up. Eventually all the stars will burn out, and all matter will collapse into dead stars and black holes. There will be no light at all. There will be no heat. There will be no life, only the corpses of dead stars and galaxies, ever–expanding into the endless darkness and the cold recesses of space, a universe in ruins. The entire universe marches irreversibly toward its grave. So not only is each individual person doomed, the entire human race is doomed. The universe is plunging toward inevitable extinction. Death is written throughout its structure. There is no escape. There is no hope. If there is no God, then man, and the universe, are doomed. Like prisoners condemned to death row, we stand and simply wait for our unavoidable execution. If there is no God, and there is no immortality, then what is the consequence of this? It means that the life that we do have is ultimately absurd. It means that the life we live is without ultimate significance, ultimate value, ultimate purpose.[4]

Suppose we think of a person's life as a series of events. Some of these events are brought about by the individual, while others are caused by external forces. Roughly, a life may be characterized as the sum total of all the things that happen to an individual while that person is alive. But, goes the argument, the value of a series of events depends entirely on the value of the very last state of affairs to which that series causally contributes. If that final outcome is valuable, then the events that led up to and contributed to it may have value. If that final state of affairs is devoid of value, then similarly all the events that led up to it are worthless.

Without God there is no afterlife of any kind. Consequently, every human life ends with the permanent cessation of the individual's conscious experience and mental activity (at least of any interesting sort). Without God, every human life terminates with the grave and the annihilation of the conscious self. The last outcome to which any human life contributes is an utterly static, lifeless, extropic, frozen universe. Since such an outcome is entirely devoid of value, it follows (according to this argument) that all human lives are entirely devoid of value and hence lack internal meaning. In a Godless universe that ends with a whimper, no human life is worth living.

A second line of reasoning is based on the idea that a life has internal meaning only if it has supernatural meaning. Suppose that your life lacks supernatural meaning. This makes you a man (or woman) without a mission. There is nothing you are supposed to be doing with your life, no higher cause you have been called to serve, no divine quest to which you have been assigned. This means that there are no criteria for evaluating whether your life is a success or a failure – which in turn implies there are no circumstances under which your life would be a successful one. Without some assigned goal, it doesn't much matter what you do: Yours is a pointless existence. A life without an externally assigned goal cannot have internal meaning. In a universe without God, without supernatural beings of any kind, there is no one suitably qualified to assign purposes to human lives. Consequently, in a universe like this, no human life can have internal meaning. We can call this the *pointless existence argument.*[5]

A third type of argument is described (and ultimately rejected) by Susan Wolf in her paper "The Meanings of Lives." Wolf writes:

> [A] life can be meaningful only if it can mean something *to* someone, and not just to *someone,* but to someone other than oneself and indeed someone of more intrinsic or ultimate value than oneself.... If there is no God, then human life, each human life, must be objectively meaningless, because if there is no God, there is no appropriate being *for whom* we could have meaning.[6]

The fundamental premise of this line of reasoning is that a life has internal meaning only if a suitably significant being cares about or takes an interest in that life. More specifically, a life has internal meaning only if an omnipotent, omniscient, morally perfect being cares about it. If no such being exists, then naturally no life is cared about by such a being, and hence no life has internal meaning. We may call this the *nobody of significance cares argument*.

A fourth and final argument, which I shall call the *God as the source of ethics argument*, is based on the idea that God must be the ultimate source of all good and evil and of all right and wrong in the universe. If God does not exist, then nothing can be good or evil and nothing can be right or wrong. Discussion of this fourth argument will be postponed to the next chapter; the remainder of this chapter deals with the first three arguments and introduces some ideas that will be helpful in the next chapter.

1.3 RICHARD TAYLOR'S WAY OUT: CREATING YOUR OWN MEANING

There are at least three interesting ways of responding to the previous three arguments. One of these is proposed by Richard Taylor (2000) in the final chapter of his book *Good and Evil*. In that chapter, titled "The Meaning of Life," Taylor discusses the case of Sisyphus, a tragic figure regularly evoked in discussions of the meaning of life. Sisyphus betrayed the gods by revealing their secrets to humankind and was sentenced to an eternity of frustration. Sisyphus was required to roll a large stone up a hill. Whenever the stone was almost at the top it would roll back down, and Sisyphus would have to begin again. Over and over, up and down the hill, went Sisyphus, accomplishing nothing. The tale is supposed to provide us with a striking example of a life devoid of internal meaning.[7]

Taylor suggests that Sisyphus' life would have internal meaning if the gods gave him a potion that filled him with an overwhelming and unending desire to roll the stone up the hill. This way Sisyphus' existence would be filled with activity of a sort he desires, and he would get to spend eternity doing exactly what he wanted to do. Moreover, this route to internal meaning is available (in principle at least) to anyone. To the question of how to make a life worth living, Taylor answers: Live in precisely the way that you most *want* to live. The chapter and the book end with these inspiring words:

You no sooner drew your first breath than you responded to the will that was in you to live. You no more ask whether it will be worthwhile, or whether anything of significance will come of it, than the worms and the birds. The point of living is simply to be living, in the manner that it is your nature to be living. . . . The meaning of life is from within us, it is not bestowed from without, and it far exceeds in both its beauty and permanence any heaven of which men have ever dreamed or yearned for.[8]

Taylor's proposal, then, is that life can have internal meaning by virtue of a correspondence between a person's desires and that person's activity. The internal value of an individual's life is directly proportional to the degree to which that individual is engaged in desired activity.[9] To the final outcome argument, Taylor would reply that looking to the final situation to which a life causally contributed is not the proper way to assess the value of that life for the one who lived it:

If the builders of a great and flourishing civilization could somehow return now to see archaeologists unearthing the trivial remnants of what they had accomplished with such effort – see the fragments of pots and vases, a few broken statues, and such tokens of another age and greatness – they could indeed ask themselves what the point of it all was, if this is what it finally came to. Yet, it did not seem so for them then, for it was just the building, and not what was built, that gave their life meaning.[10]

To the pointless existence argument, Taylor would reply that we ourselves are qualified to assign a purpose to our lives. We do not need a supernatural being to hand down such a purpose to us. A life can have internal meaning even if it lacks supernatural meaning. To the nobody of significance cares argument, Taylor would respond that *we* are sufficiently significant to make our lives meaningful. What is important is not whether God cares about your life but rather whether *you* care about it (in the appropriate way).

Taylor's view of what gives human life internal meaning has an interesting implication for philosophy. Specifically, it implies that there is a real danger involved in reflecting on the question of whether one's life has any meaning. This danger is illustrated by the case of Leo Tolstoy (2000). In *My Confession*, Tolstoy describes how, at the height of his literary success, during a time when he was "on every side surrounded by what is considered to be complete happiness," he found himself increasingly nagged by questions of whether there was any point to his life.[11] As Tolstoy reflected more and more on these questions, he began to view them with increasing seriousness:

> The questions seemed to be so foolish, simple, and childish. But the moment I touched them and tried to solve them, I became convinced, in the first place, that they were not childish and foolish, but very important and profound questions in life, and, in the second, that no matter how much I might try, I should not be able to answer them. Before attending to my Samara estate, to my son's education, or to the writing of a book, I ought to know why I should do that. So long as I did not know why, I could not do anything. I could not live.[12]

Finally, as Tolstoy describes it, he became convinced that nothing was worth doing and lost interest in everything. Tolstoy uses a parable to describe his predicament in the following powerful passage:

> Long ago has been told the Eastern story about the traveler who in the steppe is overtaken by an infuriated beast. Trying to save himself from the animal, the traveler jumps into a waterless well, but at its bottom he sees a dragon who opens his jaws in order to swallow him. And the unfortunate man does not dare climb out, lest he perish from the infuriated beast, and does not dare jump to the bottom of the well, lest he be devoured by the dragon, and so clutches the twig of a wild bush growing in a cleft of the well and holds on to it. His hands grow weak and he feels that soon he shall have to surrender to the peril which awaits him at either side; but he still holds on and sees two mice, one white, the other black, in even measure making a circle around the main trunk of the bush to which he is clinging, and nibbling at it on all sides. Now, at any moment, the bush will break and tear off, and he will fall into the dragon's jaws. The traveler sees that and knows that he will inevitably perish; but while he is still clinging, he sees some drops of honey hanging on the leaves of the bush, and so reaches out for them with his tongue and licks the leaves. Just so I hold on to the branch of life, knowing that the dragon of death is waiting inevitably for me, ready to tear me to pieces, and I cannot understand why I

have fallen on such suffering. And I try to lick that honey which used to give me pleasure; but now it no longer gives me joy . . . the honey is no longer sweet to me. I see only the inevitable dragon and the mice, and am unable to turn my glance away from them. That is not a fable, but a veritable, indisputable, comprehensible truth. . . . The two drops of honey that have longest turned my eyes away from the cruel truth, the love of family and of authorship, which I have called an art, are no longer sweet to me.[13]

In Tolstoy's case, philosophical questions and reflection caused the loss of the desire to engage in the activities that had previously sustained him. If Taylor's view about what gives life internal meaning is correct, then philosophical reflection, by taking away Tolstoy's passion for living, rendered him unable to live an internally meaningful life. If Taylor is right, then the moral of the story of Tolstoy is: Don't think too hard about whether your life has meaning, or you may find that the very pondering of the question has given the question a negative answer. Taylor also says, "[Y]ou no more ask whether it [your life] will be worthwhile, or whether anything of significance will come of it, than the worms and the birds."[14] Perhaps we should take this not as a *description* of human life but rather as a *prescription* for how to live. Socrates is famous for, among other things, his assertion that "an unexamined life is not worth living".[15] Taylor might add his own dictum: An *over*-examined life is not worth living. But can this really be right? Some detractors of philosophy might claim that devoting yourself to it entirely is a good way to render your life meaningless, but could it really be true that philosophical reflection could render all of your *other* activities worthless?

I think not; for it turns out that Taylor's view about what gives life internal meaning is mistaken. This may be seen by comparing two cases. The first case comes from an excellent article on Aristotle's views on the good life by Stephen Darwall (1999). Darwall describes a photograph that he clipped from *The New York Times*:

It shows a pianist, David Golub, accompanying two vocalists, Victoria Livengood and Erie Mills, at a tribute for Marilyn Horne. All three artists are in fine form, exercising themselves at the height of their powers. The reason I saved the photo, however, is Mr. Golub's face.

21

He is positively grinning, as if saying to himself, "And they *pay* me to do this?"[16]

Compare the case of David Golub with a variant of the case of Sisyphus: The case of the grinning excrement-eater.

The grinning excrement-eater, we may suppose, has been condemned to an eternity of eating excrement. As Taylor envisions them being merciful to Sisyphus, however, the gods have shown mercy on the excrement-eater by instilling in him a true passion for eating excrement. He gobbles it down night and day – he simply can't get enough! Both the pianist and the grinning excrement-eater are engaged in activity for which they have a genuine passion; each is doing what he most wants to do. Imagine these two lives, one filled with the sort of activity in which David Golub is engaged in Darwall's photo, the second filled with the grinning excrement-eater's favorite pastime. If we are to accept Taylor's proposal, we must conclude that both lives have internal meaning. But this conclusion is hard to swallow. If you were offered a choice between these two lives, would you be indifferent? Would the two lives seem equally worthwhile to you? If you are like me, the answer is no, in which case you must reject Taylor's proposal. It is simply going too far to say that whether a life has internal meaning is entirely a matter of the attitude of the person who lives the life.[17]

Taylor's view derives some initial plausibility from the way he introduces it. We are asked to compare a Sisyphus who hates stone-rolling with a Sisyphus who loves it. Given such a choice of Sisyphi, any rational person would prefer to be the Sisyphus to whom the gods show mercy and who comes to love stone-rolling.[18] Similarly, given a choice between a life as an excrement-eater who hates eating excrement and a life as a grinning excrement-eater, any rational person would choose the latter. Given that you have to roll stones or eat excrement for an eternity, it is better if you enjoy that sort of thing. Taylor offers a tidy explanation for these intuitions: The internal meaning of a life depends entirely on whether the agent is doing what he wants to do.

But when we make other comparisons – as between pianist Golub and the grinning excrement-eater – it becomes obvious that Taylor's proposal is faulty. A grinning excrement-eater who passes up a pianist's life for the sake of eating excrement is a fool, and if the gods get him to make such a choice by instilling in him a passion for eating excrement, then their's is a cruel joke rather than an act of mercy. No matter how great his passion, no matter how big his grin as he spoons it down, he should be an object of pity rather than of envy. If we want to find an adequate way of dealing with internal meaning we must look elsewhere.

1.4 PETER SINGER'S WAY OUT: MEANING THROUGH ELIMINATING PAIN

In the final two chapters of his book *How Are We to Live? Ethics in an Age of Self-Interest*, Peter Singer (1995) develops and defends an alternative conception of how a human life can have internal meaning. To explain Singer's view, it will be helpful to make use of the familiar distinction between *extrinsic* value on the one hand and *intrinsic* value on the other. Roughly, the intrinsic goodness (or evil) of a thing is the goodness (or evil) it has in virtue of its own nature, in and of itself.[19] In his classic work *Principia Ethica*, G. E. Moore (1903) describes a certain type of thought experiment one can use to determine the intrinsic value, if any, of a given thing. This is the so-called "isolation test," and the method is that of "considering what value we should attach to [something], if it existed in absolute isolation, stripped of all its usual accompaniments."[20] The extrinsic value of a thing, by contrast, is the value a thing has in virtue of how it is related to other things. The most familiar type of extrinsic value is *instrumental* value – the value a thing has in virtue of causing something else that is intrinsically valuable.[21]

Singer holds the view that "[w]e can live a meaningful life by working toward goals that are objectively worthwhile."[22] Singer takes *pain* to be intrinsically evil, and he maintains that the reduction of the total amount of avoidable pain in the universe is objectively

23

worthwhile. So according to Singer, one feature of at least one kind of internally meaningful life is that it reduces the overall amount of avoidable pain in the universe. But this is not a sufficient condition for internal meaningfulness. Elsewhere Singer reminds his readers of "the old wisdom that the way to find happiness or lasting satisfaction is to *aim* at something else, and *try* to do it well."[23] Later, Singer mentions "the need for a *commitment* to a cause larger than the self."[24] These passages indicate that on Singer's view, to live an internally meaningful life, one must *intend* to reduce suffering – one must have this as a conscious goal. A person who pursues only his own pleasure and accidentally reduces the total amount of suffering in the universe is not living an internally meaningful life. Although Singer does not explicitly say so, certain remarks he makes suggest that he would also hold that one must have at least some degree of *success* in achieving one's pain-reducing goal.[25] At the heart of Singer's view, then, is this principle:

(S)   An activity of S's, A, has internal meaning for S just in case (i) in doing A, S is trying to accomplish goal G, (ii) G is objectively worthwhile, and (iii) A in fact leads to G.[26]

According to Singer, one way – in fact the best way – to make your life worth living is to devote it to the reduction of avoidable pain in the universe. Singer calls this "an ethical life," and he declares that "living an ethical life enables us to identify ourselves with the grandest cause of all, and . . . is the best way open to us of making our lives meaningful."[27] Singer's view seems to be that the reduction of avoidable suffering is the most objectively worthwhile goal there is, and hence devoting one's life to it is the best way to bring internal meaning to one's life. Since this can be done whether God exists or not, the absence of God does not render all human lives internally meaningless.[28]

To establish his position, Singer adopts a method similar to the one used over two thousand years ago by Aristotle (1962) in his masterpiece *Nicomachean Ethics*. Early in the *Ethics*, Aristotle introduces three kinds of lives that humans might live: A life devoted to the pursuit of bodily pleasure; a life devoted to political activity; and a life devoted to contemplation.[29] Aristotle examines each of these and tries to determine which of the three lives is the best. For much of the *Ethics*, it appears that Aristotle has selected the life of political activity as the best, but (in a surprise move that has puzzled commentators for two and a half millennia) Aristotle ultimately selects the life of contemplation as the best.[30] In similar fashion, Singer considers a variety of activities and tries to determine which, if any, hold out the prospect of providing internal meaning. The activities Singer considers include drug and alcohol use, shopping, competition (both financial and athletic), psychotherapy, and, of course, the pursuit of the ethical life. In examining each of these, Singer seems to be concerned mainly with whether the activity produces a lasting sense of fulfillment. Singer reaches the conclusion that only the ethical life meets this condition, hence it alone (of the activities considered) can bring internal meaning to one's life.

It is important not to misunderstand what Singer is up to here. It can appear that we are back to Taylor's view that what gives a life internal meaning is simply one's attitude toward that life. Singer could be misunderstood as maintaining that what makes one's life internally meaningful is that it produces a sense of fulfillment. But Singer's position is more subtle than this. Recall the case of pianist David Golub, whose photograph Stephen Darwall described in a passage quoted in Section 1.3. The sentence immediately following the passage I quoted reads "Mr. Golub's delight is a *sign* of his activity's value, not what *makes* it good."[31] Similarly, Singer ought to be understood as viewing a lasting sense of fulfillment as a *reliable indicator* of internal meaning – much in the way that Descartes (1960) took clarity and distinctness in his ideas to be a reliable indicator of truth.[32] But what if the gods' potion gave Sisyphus a lasting sense of fulfillment as he rolled stone? And what about a fulfilled excrement-eater? Singer is not committed to the absurd conclusion that such beings live worthwhile lives. His argument does not depend on the claim that a sense of fulfillment is a reliable indicator of internal meaning in every possible world; rather, he needs only the weaker claim that it is a reliable indicator in the actual world. And in the actual world, fruitless stone-rolling and excrement-eating do not, in general, produce feelings of fulfillment, lasting or otherwise.

From time immemorial, Western philosophers have claimed that a life devoted to the acquisition of bodily pleasure is not a particularly worthwhile life for a human being to live. In the Platonic dialogue *Philebus*, Socrates imagines a creature living at the bottom of the ocean with just enough of a mind to experience mild pleasure, but utterly unable to reason, remember, or even form beliefs. Plato (1993) has Socrates say that one who lived such a life "would thus not live a human life but the life of a mollusk or one of those creatures in shells that live in the sea."[33] Aristotle characterizes a life devoted to bodily pleasure as "a life suitable to cattle."[34] Elsewhere he says that "even a slave, can enjoy bodily pleasures. . . . But no one would grant that a slave has a share in happiness."[35] Aristotle thought of slaves as less than fully human. The consensus, then, of the two greatest ancient Greek philosophers is that a life devoted to pleasure might be acceptable for mollusks, cows, and sub-humans, but it is no way for a human being to live.[36] The tradition continues in the twentieth century with Robert Nozick's (1977) well-known example of "the experience machine," a virtual reality device that produces any desired experience in the mind of someone hooked up to it. Nozick says: "We learn that something matters to us in addition to experience by imagining an experience machine and then realizing that we would not use it."[37]

Even those philosophers traditionally associated with hedonism are careful to make clear that it is not the unbridled pursuit of bodily pleasure alone that they recommend. Epicurus (1964), for example, in his "Letter to Menoeceus" writes:

> When we say that pleasure is the end, we do not mean the pleasure of the profligate or that which depends on physical enjoyment – as some think who do not understand our teachings, disagree with them, or give them an evil interpretation – but by pleasure we mean the state wherein the body is free from pain and the mind from anxiety.[38]

Similarly, in *Utilitarianism*, John Stuart Mill (1979), defending utilitarianism against the charge that it is a "doctrine worthy only of swine," notes that there are different qualities of pleasure, and that bodily pleasure is of the lowest quality and hence is the least valuable kind of pleasure: "[T]here is no known Epicurean theory of life which does not assign to the pleasures of the intellect, of the feelings and imagination, and of the moral sentiments a much higher value as pleasures than to those of mere sensation."[39]

At this point it might be objected that, at least for the purposes of Singer's argument, the testimony of all these philosophers should not be given much weight. After all, they are *philosophers* – precisely the sort of people who *haven't* devoted their lives to the pursuit of bodily pleasure. Wouldn't the testimony of those who have pursued pleasure be more relevant to the question of whether such a life can bring lasting fulfillment?

One of the strengths of Singer's argument is that he considers the testimony of those who have devoted themselves to the various activities he discusses. I will not repeat all of Singer's examples here, but one of the most remarkable bits of testimony comes from Tom Landry, the extremely successful coach of professional football's Dallas Cowboys:

> ...Even after you've just won the Super Bowl – *especially* after you've just won the Super Bowl – *there's always next year*. If 'Winning isn't everything. It's the only thing', then 'the only thing' is nothing – emptiness, the nightmare of a life without ultimate meaning.[40]

One piece of interesting testimony not discussed by Singer comes from an infamous devotee of bodily pleasure – the Marquis de Sade (1992). Here is a man who surely has some insight into whether the pursuit of bodily pleasure can bring lasting fulfillment! In de Sade's story *Justine*, the heroine falls into the hands of four lascivious friars who hold her captive and take advantage of her. It is telling that de Sade has one of the friars make the following remark to Justine:

> Spending the night with one woman always makes me want another in the morning. Nothing is quite as insatiable as our urges; the greater the offerings we make to them, the hotter they burn. Of course, the outcome is always pretty much the same, yet we always imagine that there is better just around the corner. The instant our thirst for one

27

woman is slaked is also the moment when the same drives kindle our desire for another.[41]

The similarity between these remarks and the remarks of Tom Landry is striking. In both cases we get a portrait of men driven by relentless desires that reappear the instant they are satisfied. More significantly, a sense of fulfillment seems to be entirely absent: The desires reappear, often stronger than before, precisely because the satisfaction of the previous desire fails to yield fulfillment.

Turning to the ethical life, Singer discusses the cases of Henry Spira, a life-long activist, and Christine Townend, who, together with her husband, sold her expensive house and flew off to India for five years of volunteer work. According to Singer, both find fulfillment in their devotion to the ethical life. Of Spira, Singer writes: "When, on my occasional visits to New York, I stay with him and his cat in his Upper Westside rent-controlled apartment, I always find him thinking about strategies for getting things moving ahead, and relishing the next challenge. I leave in good spirits."[42] Like Taylor's book, Singer's ends with an inspiring message. Indeed, it is clear that Singer is calling for a kind of ethical revolution:

> If 10 percent of the population were to take a consciously ethical outlook on life and act accordingly, the resulting change would be more significant than any change of government.... Anyone can become part of the critical mass that offers us a chance of improving the world before it is too late.... You will find plenty of worthwhile things to do. You will not be bored, or lack fulfillment in your life. Most important of all, you will know that you have not lived and died for nothing, because you will have become part of the great tradition of those who have responded to the amount of pain and suffering in the universe by trying to make the world a better place.[43]

In response to the pointless existence argument, Singer, like Taylor, would reply that we do not need a supernaturally bestowed purpose for our lives to have internal meaning. But Singer's basis for this claim is different from Taylor's. Singer's claim is that the presence of avoidable intrinsic evil in the universe takes the place of a supernatural commander as the thing that renders our lives internally meaningful: "There is a tragic irony in the fact that we can find our own fulfillment precisely because there is so much avoidable pain and suffering in the universe, but that is the way the world is."[44] Similarly, it does not matter whether an omnipotent, omniscient, morally perfect being cares about our lives or not. Preventing suffering is worthwhile regardless of whether there is any such being around to pay attention to it. So we should not be concerned by the nobody significant cares argument. In response to the final outcome argument, Singer would reply that such an argument arbitrarily places an undue amount of importance – indeed *all* of the importance – on the *final* state of affairs to which a life leads. But why single out the very last outcome as the only one that matters?

> Suppose that we become involved in a project to help a small community in a developing country to become free of debt and self–sufficient in food. The project is an outstanding success, and the villagers are healthier, happier, better educated, economically secure, and have fewer children. Now someone might say: 'What good have you done? In a thousand years these people will all be dead, and their children and grandchildren as well, and nothing that you have done will make any difference.' ... We should not, however, think of our efforts as wasted unless they endure forever, or even for a very long time. If we regard time as a fourth dimension, then we can think of the universe, throughout all the times at which it contains sentient life, as a four–dimensional entity. We can then make that four–dimensional world a better place by causing there to be less pointless suffering in one particular place, at one particular time, than there would otherwise have been.... We will have had a positive effect on the universe.[45]

Regardless of whether we accept all that Singer has to say, we are now in a position to see that the final outcome argument fails. That argument fails because it is based on what Paul Edwards (2000) calls a "curious and totally arbitrary preference of the future to the present."[46] There are a variety of ways of assessing the relative importance of various times. Singer suggests that we ought to view them as being of equal importance. Another view ranks the present and the near future as most important. This point of view lies behind the now-clichéd command to "seize the day." Yes, death awaits us all, and in the end we will turn to nothing more than food for worms – but the proper reaction to this fact is not to give up but rather to get moving! Marcus Aurelius (1805) expressed this idea in the second century c.e. this way: "Do not act as if you had ten thousand years to throw away. Death stands at your elbow."[47] A third perspective views the final moments of time (or, if time has no end, the final *outcome*) as the most important, and it is this perspective that lies behind the final outcome argument. But of the three perspectives, the last is surely the *least* reasonable. A diagnosis of why this manner of thinking can seem reasonable comes later, but for now it is sufficient to see that it is not. Returning to Singer's remarks, the proper response to the question what good have you done? is I've made these villagers happier than they would have been otherwise – and what things will be like a thousand years from now is utterly irrelevant to this fact. Isn't it better that the Nazi Holocaust ended when it did rather than in, say, 1970 – regardless of what the world will be like a million years from now? I can remember occasions in junior high gym class when a basketball or volleyball game became particularly heated and adolescent tempers flared. Our gym teacher sometimes attempted to calm us down with such rhetorical questions as, "Ten years from now, will any of you care who won this game?" It always struck me that a reasonable response to such a query would be, "Does it really matter *now* whether any of us will care in ten years?" In much the same vein, Thomas Nagel (1979) suggests that "it does not matter now that in a million years nothing we do now will matter."[48]

There are many questions that might be asked about Singer's position. Is a sense of fulfillment really a reliable indicator of internal meaning? Is the ethical life as it is characterized by Singer really the *best* way to bring internal meaning to one's life? With respect to the second question, consider that the painless annihilation of all life would drastically reduce the amount of avoidable suffering in the universe – yet surely Singer would not endorse this as an objectively worthwhile goal! Perhaps the ethical life needs to be characterized a bit more carefully. Nevertheless, Singer's position is superior to Taylor's in at least one respect: It provides a straightforward and plausible model that allows us to reject the first three internal meaning arguments from the Section 1.2. At the heart of Singer's view is the idea that committing oneself to making the universe a better place overall – increasing the amount of intrinsic goodness in the universe (or decreasing the amount of intrinsic evil) – can bring internal meaning to one's life. Since one can do this even if one's life lacks supernatural meaning, and no omnipotent being cares about one's life, and the *final* outcome to which one's life will contribute is valueless, it follows that the final outcome argument, the nobody of significance cares argument, and the pointless existence argument all fail.

1.5 ARISTOTLE'S WAY OUT: INTRINSICALLY GOOD ACTIVITY

A third view suggests another way of responding to these arguments. This view is the oldest, simplest, and perhaps the most powerful of the responses considered in this chapter. It is found in Aristotle's *Nicomachean Ethics* – and one doesn't have to read very far to find it. The *Ethics* begins with these lines:

> Every art or applied science and every systematic investigation, and similarly every action and choice, seem to aim at some good. . . . But it is clear that there is a difference in the ends at which they aim: in some cases the activity is the end, in others the end is some product beyond the activity.[49]

At the end of this passage Aristotle divides activities into two categories – those that are good because of what they produce, and those that are good in and of themselves. In this brief remark, Aristotle suggests a possibility not considered by either Taylor or Singer. It is a simple yet profound insight:

Aristotle's Insight: Some activities are *intrinsically good*.

Activities of this sort are worth engaging in *even if they lead to nothing of value*. They would be worthwhile even if they had no consequences at all. This suggests a third way of bringing internal meaning to one's life: Engage in intrinsically good activities, activities that are worth doing for their own sake. It is part of the very nature of such activities to bring internal meaning to one's life.

In his surprise ending to the *Ethics*, Aristotle singles out contemplation (*theoria*) as the activity with the greatest amount of intrinsic value.[50] This activity may be very roughly characterized as reflection on the basic nature of the universe. This activity is not the acquisition of knowledge; rather, it is reflection upon what one already knows. One of the more interesting arguments Aristotle offers to support his claim that this is the best sort of activity goes like this:

> We assume that the gods are in the highest degree blessed and happy. But what kind of actions are we to attribute to them? Acts of justice? Will they not look ridiculous making contracts with one another, returning deposits, and so forth? Perhaps acts of courage – withstanding terror and taking risks, because it is noble to do so? Or generous actions? But to whom will they give? It would be strange to think that they actually have currency or something of the sort. Acts of self–control? What would they be? Surely, it would be in poor taste to praise them for not having bad appetites. If we went through the whole list we would see that a concern with actions is petty and unworthy of the gods. Nevertheless, we all assume that the gods exist and, consequently, that they are active; for surely we do not assume them to be always asleep. . . . Now, if we take away action from a living being, to say nothing of production, what is left except contemplation? Therefore, the activity of the divinity which surpasses all others in bliss must be a contemplative activity, and the human activity which is most closely akin to it is, therefore, most conducive to happiness.[51]

Whatever activity the gods engage in is intrinsically the best kind of activity. The gods must engage only in contemplation; therefore, contemplation must intrinsically be the best kind of activity. Thus, Aristotle singles out for the highest praise the activity of the successful philosopher – reflection on what he has learned. In reaching this conclusion, Aristotle outdoes his great teacher, Plato. In the *Republic*, Plato had argued that philosophers *ought* to be *kings*.[52] Aristotle goes further to suggest that philosophers *are* like *gods*. Alone among the great stinking masses of humanity, philosophers are capable, at least briefly, of rising above their place in the universe and doing the sort of thing that normally is reserved for the gods. It is clear that in the Aristotelian universe philosophers hold a special place indeed!

There is an interesting contrast worth noting between the view expressed here by the great pagan philosopher and the Christian tradition. Aristotle praises the attempt to transcend one's station in the universe and to become like the gods. But according to one strand of thought in the Christian tradition, this sort of thing is harshly condemned. Indeed, according to traditional Christianity, it is precisely this sort of thing that led to the Fall of Man. For instance, in John Milton's (1956) classic *Paradise Lost,* the angel Raphael warns Adam against probing the secrets of the universe:

> But whether these things, or whether not, / Whether the sun predominant in heaven / Rise on the earth, or earth rise on the sun, / ... Solicit not thy thoughts with matters hid; / Leave them to God above, him serve and fear; / ... Think only what concerns thee and thy being; / Dream not of other worlds, what creatures there / Contented that thus far hath been reveal'd / Not of earth only, but of highest heav'n.[53]

Later, the serpent convinces Eve to eat the fruit from the Tree of Knowledge by telling her that if she and Adam eat the fruit "ye shall be as gods / Knowing both good and evil as they know".[54] And, of course, it is Eve's eating of the fruit that leads to disaster for all of humanity. The message is clear: Mind your own business, be grateful for what God has revealed to you, and, whatever you do, do not, under any circumstances, attempt to transcend your station in the universe.

What, then, are we to make of Aristotle's proposal that contemplation is intrinsically the best sort of activity? In his discussion of the case of Sisyphus, Richard Taylor considers a scenario in which the wretched man's labors *do* produce something. Taylor imagines that Sisyphus' efforts are directed toward the production of a beautiful and enduring temple, and he writes:

> And let us suppose he succeeded in this, that after ages of dreadful toil, all directed at this final result, he did at last complete his temple, such that now he could say his work was done, and he could rest and forever enjoy the result. Now what? What picture now presents itself to our minds? It is precisely the picture of infinite boredom! Of Sisyphus doing nothing ever again, but contemplating what he has

already wrought and can no longer add anything to, and contemplating it for an eternity![55]

Taylor suggests that contemplation of the completed temple would be no more worthwhile than Sisyphus' pointless uphill toil in the original version of the story, and I am inclined to agree. Furthermore, the contemplation that Aristotle praises seems to me to have much in common with Sisyphus' contemplation of his completed temple. I don't see much intrinsic worth in either activity. If the gods who condemned Sisyphus were gods of the sort Aristotle envisions, then the fate to which they condemned him was no worse than their own.

Still, even if we reject the details of Aristotle's proposal, we can accept Aristotle's insight. If there are activities available to us during our lifetimes that are intrinsically valuable, then our lives can have internal meaning even if God does not exist. Even if there is no supernatural commander to assign purposes to our lives or a suitably Significant Deity to care about our lives, the existence of intrinsically good activities would make it possible for us to bring internal meaning to our lives. I submit that there are such activities.

What are some intrinsically good activities? And how can I prove that my favored list is the right one? As to the first question, I have nothing particularly insightful or novel to say: My list of intrinsically good activities would include falling in love, engaging in intellectually stimulating activity, being creative in various ways, experiencing pleasure of various kinds, and teaching.[56] To my list it might be objected: Aren't you simply listing things you happen to enjoy doing? The answer is no. There are plenty of things I enjoy doing but do not consider intrinsically worthwhile, and I suspect that a bit of reflection will reveal that the same is true of you. In my own case, playing video games fits the bill. For many years now I have had a passion for video games, and I can spend hour after hour playing them. But I do not regard this activity as intrinsically worthwhile, and I think that a life devoted entirely to it would be a wasted one. In fact, precisely because I enjoy it so much and yet consider it intrinsically worthless, I intentionally refrain from purchasing home video game systems and from installing games on my computer. I know that if video games were readily available to me I would waste countless hours on this frivolous pastime. So the list of activities that I consider to have intrinsic worth is not the same as the list of activities I enjoy.

And how can I justify my list of intrinsically worthwhile activities? I am afraid I have no philosophical proof for, say, the proposition that falling in love is intrinsically good. As has often been pointed out, though, many of the things we know are such that we cannot give an adequate philosophical proof for their truth. The method I recommend for deciding which activities are intrinsically good is a version of G. E. Moore's isolation test described in Section 1.4: To see if an activity is intrinsically good, consider whether you would find it worthwhile *even if it had absolutely no consequences*. If it seems to you that it *would* be worthwhile, then you have a good candidate for an intrinsically good activity on your hands. Claims about what is intrinsically good are the axioms of ethical theory; they are the starting points, the first principles. As such, they are unlikely to be the sorts of things that can be *proved*. Nevertheless, it is perfectly consistent to say that some activities are intrinsically valuable – and that we *know* what some of these are.

Aristotle's distinction between activities that are good because of what they produce and activities that are intrinsically good helps us to understand why the final outcome argument can seem convincing even though, as I contend, it is a bad argument. The final outcome argument can be made to seem convincing by focusing on activities that are not intrinsically good. If one becomes convinced that all the activities available to us in our earthly lives are of this sort, then the final outcome of all these activities can seem to be of the utmost importance. The reason is that, convinced that the activities that make up our lives are intrinsically worthless, we may believe that the only way they can be worthwhile at all is if they lead to a worthwhile final outcome. Toward the beginning of this chapter I quoted from William Lane Craig's talk "The Absurdity of Life Without God." In that same talk Craig discusses Beckett's play *Waiting for Godot*. Craig uses the play to explain what he thinks human life would be like without God: "During this entire play, two men carry on trivial, mind–numbing, banal conversation while waiting for a third man to arrive who never does. And our lives are like that, Beckett is saying. We just kill time waiting. For what? We don't know."[57]

Notice that the activity in this example is trivial, mind-numbing, and banal. The activity Beckett singles out is obviously *intrinsically* worthless: Any worth it might have would derive only from the arrival of Godot. Because Godot never shows, up the activity is altogether worthless. In likening all of human life to the play, Craig implies that all the activities available to us during our earthly lives are intrinsically worthless. In fact, this is the unstated assumption underlying each of the internal meaning arguments we have been discussing. All three arguments assume that no activity available to us on earth has any intrinsic value. Such activities can have value only if it is bestowed on them from the outside – by being part of a divine plan or an object of concern on the part of a Significant Deity, or by leading to something else of value. But it is precisely this assumption that should be rejected. If the characters waiting for Godot had been in the process of falling in love with each other, would the fact that Godot never showed up have rendered their activity worthless – would the entire evening have been a complete waste? Hardly.

Recall Tolstoy's example of the traveler who falls into a well. The nature of the traveler's predicament depends on what activities are available to him while he is trapped. Recall another part of the story: The traveler sees some drops of honey hanging from a bush and reaches out and licks them. In likening his own situation to that of the trapped traveler, Tolstoy added the proviso that "the honey is no longer sweet to me" – that is, none of the activities available to him had any intrinsic worth.[58]

Ask yourself this question: If you found yourself in the traveler's predicament, would you have a preference concerning the presence or absence of honey? If the final outcome argument is correct, it should not matter to you. But I suspect you are like me and you do have a preference for honey. As a matter of contingent fact, some humans may be unable to engage in activities that are intrinsically good: They may be like travelers trapped in the well with no honey in sight. But this is hardly an essential feature of the human condition. Since you are reading this book it is likely that you do not face such a situation. There is honey all around you; you have but to reach out and lick it. You do not need God to give your life internal meaning.[59]

The main character of the Spike Jonze (2002) film *Adaptation* is Charlie Kaufman, a screenwriter trying to write a screenplay based on Susan Orlean's book *The Orchid Thief*. At one point in the film, Kaufman, struggling to complete his script, attends a screenwriting seminar. During the seminar Kaufman raises his hand and asks the following question: "[W]hat if a writer is attempting to create a story where nothing much happens, where people don't change, they don't have any epiphanies. They struggle and are frustrated and nothing is resolved. More a reflection of the real world. . . . " Kaufman is unable to complete his question because he is interrupted by the seminar's leader. The speaker's response can be construed as a response to Craig and Tolstoy in the spirit of Singer and Aristotle. It also serves as a fitting end to this chapter:

> Nothing happens in the real world? Are you out of your f***ing mind? People are murdered every day! There's genocide and war and corruption! Every f***ing day somewhere in the world somebody sacrifices his life to save someone else! Every f***ing day someone somewhere makes a conscious decision to destroy someone else! People find love: People lose it, for Christ's sake! A child watches her mother beaten to death on the steps of a church! Someone goes hungry! Somebody else betrays his best friend for a woman! If you can't find that stuff in life, then you, my friend don't know much about life![60]

TWO

GOD AND MORALITY

"[W]hat's beloved by the gods is pious, and what's not beloved by
them is impious."

– Euthyphro[1]

2.1 GOD AS THE OMNIPOTENT CREATOR OF ETHICS

Theists often hold that ethics is, in some fashion, dependent upon the
existence or activity of God. There are countless ways of understanding the precise nature of this dependence; this chapter is devoted to
exploring some of these. One particularly strong version of this idea
holds that God is the *omnipotent creator* of ethics. Let us consider this
idea in some detail.

All existing entities may be divided into two categories. The first
contains all and only those things that are such that it is possible for
them not to exist. These things have a *contingent existence*.[2] Consider,
for instance, the very book that you are reading now. Eventually it
will cease to exist. Moreover, its author might have been killed before
its completion, in which case it never would have existed at all. The
second category contains all and only those things that are such that
it is impossible for them not to exist. Things in this category simply
must exist and hence are said to have *necessary existence*.[3] Uncontro-
versial examples of items in this category are harder to come by.
Numbers might fit the bill, or Platonic forms (if there are any such
things). According to one traditional way of thinking about God,
God would fall into this category. Truths may be similarly divided

into those that are contingently true (are true but could fail to be true) and those that are necessarily true (*must* be true). Contingent truths include facts such as our solar system contains exactly nine planets, the earth orbits the sun, and the speed of light is 299,792,458 meters per second. Necessary truths are typically thought to contain, among other things, truths of logic (for example, p implies p) and mathematical truths (such as $2 + 2 = 4$).

Theists typically maintain that God is the omnipotent creator of the universe. This thesis usually is understood as implying at least that God is the ultimate source of all contingently existing things and of all contingent truths. Some theists hold that God's creative powers extend not just to the way the universe is and the things that it contains, but also to the way the universe ought to be and the values it contains. Philip Quinn (1998) explains this approach nicely:

> Theists customarily wish to insist on a sharp distinction between God and the world, between the creator and the created realm. According to traditional accounts of creation and conservation, each contingent thing depends on God's power for its existence whenever it exists. God, by contrast, depends on nothing external to himself for his existence. So God has complete sovereignty over contingent existence. . . . Considerations of theoretical unity of a familiar sort then make it attractive to extend the scope of divine sovereignty . . . from the realm of fact into the realm of value.[4]

Theists who hold the sort of view described by Quinn maintain that just as it is God's creative activity that brought it about that atoms exist and that light has the speed it does, it is also God's creative activity that determines which things are good and evil, which actions are morally right, wrong, and obligatory, which traits of character are virtues and vices, which human lives are worth living, and so on. According to a particularly strong version of this view, God has the power to arrange morality as He sees fit; He is the author of the laws of morality in the same sense that He is the author of the laws of nature. Moreover, because He is omnipotent, the only constraint on which laws of morality God creates is the limit of possibility. If we understand *ethical claims* as claims about which things are good, evil, morally right, wrong, obligatory, virtuous, or vicious, then we can capture the essence of this view with the following pair of theses:[5]

Control Thesis: Every *logically consistent* ethical claim, E, is such that God could make E true.[6]

Dependency Thesis: Every *true* ethical claim is true in virtue of some act of will on the part of God.

The Dependency Thesis may be held as a contingent truth or as a necessary truth. If it is a necessary truth, then the presence of ethical truths in the universe entails that God exists. If the thesis is necessarily true then without God, nothing can be good, bad, right, wrong, virtuous, or vicious. As Craig puts it, "In a universe without God, good and evil do not exist. There is only the bare, valueless, fact of existence."[7] This sort of argument – from the premise that the Dependency Thesis is necessarily true to the conclusion that there are no ethical truths if God does not exist – is the *God as the source of ethics* argument.[8]

Some theists who accept the conclusion of the God as the source of ethics argument fail to appreciate its consequences fully. Craig is an example. One of his central themes is how *awful* it would be if God did not exist. Consider, for instance, Craig's account of the realization of his own mortality:

> I can remember very vividly the first time my father told me, as a child, that someday, I was going to die. Somehow as a child the thought had just never occurred to me, and when he told me, I was just over-whelmed with an unbearable fear and sadness, and I cried and cried and cried, and although my father tried to reassure me repeatedly that this event was a long way off, to me that just didn't matter. The fact was that I was going to die and would be no more. And that thought just overwhelmed me.[9]

Later, Craig refers to the "horror of modern man" – facing life in (what "modern man" takes to be) a Godless universe. But if there can be no good or evil if God does not exist, then there can be no *evil* if God does not exist. So if God doesn't exist, nothing *bad* can ever happen to anyone. The conclusion of the God as the source of ethics argument implies that there is nothing good about a Godless universe – but it equally implies that there is nothing *bad* about it either. If this argument is sound there can be nothing awful or horrible about a Godless universe. The short version of Craig's self-contradictory message is "Without God there would be no value in the universe – and think how horrible that would be!"

Still, this confusion by itself does not constitute an objection to the God as the source of ethics argument. To criticize that argument, I will consider two positions. The stronger position consists of both the Control Thesis and the Dependency Thesis. The weaker position denies the Control Thesis but accepts the Dependency Thesis. Ultimately I will conclude that both theses are false. If this is right, then the God as the source of ethics argument fails.

Since the God as the source of ethics argument relies only on the Dependency Thesis, some might wonder why I bother to discuss the Control Thesis at all. One reason is my suspicion that some theists may find the Dependency Thesis attractive because they accept the Control Thesis. Although the latter does not entail the former, acceptance of the latter naturally suggests acceptance of the former. Another reason is that the fact that the Control Thesis is false is an important piece of information that will help us understand properly the relationship between God and ethical truth. After criticizing both the strong and the weak positions, I will sketch an alternative account of God's relationship to ethical truth. The earlier rejection of both the strong and weak positions will help to motivate this account.

2.2 CRITICISM OF THE STRONG POSITION

One difficulty with the Control Thesis can be illustrated by a simple example. Imagine a contest in which the prize is omnipotence. There are two competitors in this contest. The first competitor hopes to win the prize and use his omnipotence for the good of humanity. He intends to bring peace, justice, and happiness to the entire world. The second competitor hopes to win the prize and use his omnipotence for his own selfish, nefarious purposes. He plans to slaughter most of humanity and force the rest to live in excrement pits where they will work themselves to death as his slaves and be subject to torture at his hand for his amusement. As it happens, the second competitor wins the contest and becomes omnipotent. It seems clear that the worst has happened – a thoroughly vicious being has become all-powerful and the world is on the verge of being plunged into evil. Fortunately, this does not happen. This is because the first use to which the winner puts his newly acquired omnipotence is to change certain ethical facts. He makes it the case that the slaughter of innocents is fantastically good, that undeserved suffering is just, and that a human life devoted to serving him has the greatest possible amount of internal meaning. He also makes it the case that he himself is a morally perfect being. He does this not by changing the nature of his character (his desires, motives, goals, and so on are just the same as before), but rather by *changing the nature of moral perfection*. He then implements his now fantastically good and just plan. He slaughters most of the humans, throws the rest into the pits, and so on. But, because he changed the ethical facts first, the story has a happy ending. All is for the best. The film version of this scenario would leave you grinning like a fool as you left the theater.

There is just one problem with all of this: The story in question is crazy. What is crazy about the story is precisely the idea that a being could be powerful enough to make it the case that, for instance, the slaughter of innocents is fantastically good. There simply is no amount of power that would enable a being to make that true. Power – even omnipotence – may be used in the service of good or evil, but its use is to be evaluated within a moral framework that is itself not subject to the power in question. This story seems to get things backward by making morality subject to power. We might put the point this way: A (putatively) moral framework that could be completely rearranged by a sufficiently powerful being is not a *moral* framework at all. The moral of this story is that omnipotence does not include power over all ethical claims. But presumably if the Control Thesis is true at all, it is true in virtue of the fact that omnipotence does include this sort of power. Hence, the Control Thesis is false.

Some theists may be willing to bite the bullet here and accept that, strange as it may seem, the story told above is at least a coherent one. But I think there is another reason for a theist to reject the Control

42

Thesis. This reason has to do with the problem of evil. This ancient challenge to Christianity alleges that an omnipotent, omniscient, and morally perfect God would not permit the presence of evil in the world. Since there is evil in the world, it follows that God does not exist. In *Dialogues Concerning Natural Religion*, Hume puts the problem into the mouth of the character of Philo: "Is he willing to prevent evil, but not able? then is he impotent. Is he able, but not willing? then is he malevolent. Is he both able and willing? whence then is evil?"[10]

Christian philosophers through the ages have sought to address this challenge. But many of the most promising responses to the challenge turn out to be inconsistent with the Control Thesis. To illustrate this point we must examine some ways of responding to the problem of evil.

One popular response to the problem of evil is the *free will defense*. The most well-known contemporary version of the free will defense is probably Alvin Plantinga's version. (Plantinga develops his version in part as a response to some claims made by John Mackie (1992), so it will be useful to begin with Mackie's remarks). Mackie understands the free will defense as an attempt to show that God would permit some evil in the world because this is the only way He could create a world in which there are creatures with free will. This is so because free will entails evil and "it is better on the whole that men should act freely, and sometimes err, than that they should be innocent automata, acting rightly in a wholly determined way."[11] As Mackie understands it, then, the free will defense consists of the claims that (1) the presence of free creatures in the universe entails the presence of evil in the universe, and (2) free will is a great good and its presence in the universe outweighs a certain amount of evil. Mackie's main criticism of the free will defense is straightforward: "God was not ... faced with a choice between making innocent automata and making beings who, in acting freely, would sometimes go wrong: there was open to him the obviously better possibility of making beings who would act freely but always go right."[12] Mackie rejects part (1) of the free will defense as he understands it and offers the following counterargument:

Mackie's Criticism of the Free Will Defense

1. It is possible that there are beings who are free to choose between right and wrong and always freely do the right thing.
2. An omnipotent God could bring about any possible situation.
3. Therefore, an omnipotent God could bring it about that there are beings who are free to choose between right and wrong and always freely do the right thing.

Plantinga responds to Mackie's criticism by presenting a version of the free will defense that implies that the second premise of Mackie's criticism is false. Plantinga seeks to establish that it is *possible* that God, despite being omnipotent, is unable to create the best of all possible worlds.[13] And Plantinga's version of the free will defense implies that, under any circumstances, there are possible situations that even an omnipotent God cannot bring about.[14]

One of the key assumptions underlying Plantinga's defense is that there is, for every creature that God could have created, and for every situation in which that creature could have found itself, a fact of the matter as to what that creature would have *freely* done had it been in the situation in question and been able to choose freely between right and wrong.[15] Plantinga holds, furthermore, that these facts – the so-called true *counterfactuals of creaturely freedom* – are not under God's control. Which ones are true is not up to God; He simply finds Himself stuck with a certain set of true counterfactuals of freedom and must do the best He can within those constraints. The essence, then, of Plantinga's free will defense is the possibility that the truth values of these counterfactuals will come out in such a way that God is simply unable to give *anyone* a free choice between right and wrong without *someone* doing something wrong. Under such circumstances God would be unable to create a universe in which there are creatures who are able to choose freely between right and wrong and in which there is no evil. To see how this might happen we may consider the following simple model.

Suppose there are just two creatures, Bill and Ted, that God could create and two possible situations, S1 and S2, in which these creatures could be placed. Suppose that in S1 there are two possible courses of action, A1 and A2, and in S2 there are two courses of action, A3 and A4. A1 and A3 are morally wrong; A2 and A4 are morally right. Suppose the following counterfactuals turn out to be true:

1. If Bill only were in S1, he would freely perform A1.
2. If Ted only were in S1, he would freely perform A1.
3. If Bill only were in S2, he would freely perform A3.
4. If Ted only were in S2, he would freely perform A3.
5. If Bill and Ted were in S1 together, Bill would freely perform A1.
6. If Bill and Ted were in S2 together, Bill would freely perform A3.[16]

Given these true counterfactuals there is no way God can give anyone the freedom to choose between right and wrong without someone doing something wrong.[17] Plantinga's idea is that the very same thing *could* happen in a model that matches the actual world – one which presumably contains infinitely many possible creatures, situations, and actions. And were this to occur, God would be similarly stuck; He couldn't create a world with free creatures and no evil. (We might imagine a harried and frustrated God considering the various counterfactuals, shaking his head and muttering to himself as He traces through the infinite possibilities.)[18]

But this entire picture falls apart if the Control Thesis is true. This is because the free will defense relies on the tacit assumption that there are certain ethical truths that are not under God's control. To see this, consider Plantinga's preliminary statement of his free will defense:

A world containing free creatures who are significantly free (and freely perform more good than evil actions) is more valuable, all else being equal, than a world containing no free creatures at all. Now God can create free creatures, but He can't *cause* or *determine* them to do only what is right. For if He does so, then they aren't significantly free after all; they do not do what is right *freely*.... As it turned out, sadly enough, some of the free creatures God created went wrong in the exercise of their freedom; this is the source of moral evil. The fact that free creatures sometimes go wrong, however, counts neither against God's omnipotence nor against His goodness; for He could have forestalled the occurrence of moral evil only by removing the possibility of moral good.[19]

Notice how the passage begins. Plantinga claims that significant freedom (the freedom to choose between right and wrong) is a great good. It is so good, in fact, that it is worth permitting a certain amount of evil in the world in order to bring in morally significant freedom. But suppose, as the Control Thesis implies, that it is within God's power to make it the case that morally significant freedom is *not* a great good – indeed, that it is not good at all. Moreover, if the Control Thesis is true, it is within God's power to make it the case that the causally determined, non-free performance of morally right actions is a great good. Therefore, if the Control Thesis is true, then Plantinga's free will defense utterly fails to establish that God *could* have been justified in permitting evil in the world because doing so was the only way He could introduce a great good. If, as the Control Thesis implies, it is up to God to decide *which things are great goods*, then God is not stuck with the claim that freedom is better than causal determination. But Plantinga's defense works only if God is stuck with this claim. Therefore, Plantinga's free will defense succeeds only if the Control Thesis is false.

A second prominent contemporary response to the problem of evil is John Hick's (1966) "vale of soul-making" response. Hick's response is based on the idea that the primary purpose of this world is to make a certain kind of moral transformation possible for human beings. God designed the world in such a way as to enable us to become beings of a certain type. Hick describes the idea this way:

> [M]an, created as a personal being in the image of God, is only the raw material for a further and more difficult stage of God's creative work. This is the leading of men as relatively free and autonomous persons, through their own dealings with life in the world in which He has placed them, towards that quality of personal existence that is the finite likeness of God. The features of this likeness are revealed in the person of Christ. . . . [20]

What God wants – and the purpose for which He designed the world – is for human beings to transform themselves into Christ-like beings by way of their own free choices. This transformation requires that humans face and overcome various forms of evil; this is why our world contains evil. And, once we understand the true purpose of this world, we will be in a position to assess its value accurately: "[T]his world must be a place of soul–making. And its value is to be judged, not primarily by the quantity of pleasure and pain occurring in it at any particular moment, but by its fitness for its primary purpose, the purpose of soul–making."[21] As in the case of Plantinga's free will defense, the Control Thesis undermines Hick's view. This is because, like Plantinga's, Hick's view depends on the assumption that there are ethical facts over which God has no control. Hick writes:

> The value–judgement that is implicitly being invoked here is that one who has attained to goodness by meeting and eventually mastering temptations, and thus by rightly making responsible choices in concrete situations, is good in a richer and more valuable sense than would be one created *ab initio* in a state either of innocence or of moral virtue.[22]

Hick's response assumes that a being who has become virtuous through free choice is *better* than one who, from the start, was simply created virtuous. But the Control Thesis implies that God could have made it the case that a being who is created virtuous initially is better than one who has become virtuous through free choice. And if God could have done this, then Hick's response fails. Therefore, like Plantinga's response, Hick's response succeeds only if the Control Thesis is false.

The responses to the problem of evil by Plantinga and Hick both fit the following schema:

> There is some thing, G, such that (a) G is a great good and (b) it may be (or is) the case that God cannot introduce G into the world without also permitting some evil in the world. Therefore, God may be (or is) justified in permitting some evil in the world.[23]

But if the Control Thesis is true, then no response that follows this schema can work, since: (1) for any great good G, God has the power to make it the case that G is not a great good; and (2) There are plenty of things that do not satisfy condition (b) above that God could have made great goods. Causally determined beings who always nonfreely do the right thing and beings who are created virtuous from the start are examples. If the Control Thesis is true, God can never be forced to introduce evil into the world in order to secure a greater good, since there is always open to Him the alternative of producing something that can be created without introducing evil into the world and making that other thing a great good.

2.3 CRITICISM OF THE WEAK POSITION

There are, then, good reasons for theist and naturalist alike to reject the Control Thesis. However, even if this is right, it doesn't refute the God as the source of ethics argument because that argument is based on the Dependency Thesis. Moreover, some theists have proposed a way of rejecting the Control Thesis while continuing to hold the Dependency Thesis. We may broach this proposal by way of an objection to the Strong Position proposed by Ralph Cudworth (1976):

> [D]iverse modern theologers do not only seriously, but zealously contend...that there is nothing absolutely, intrinsically, and naturally good and evil, just and unjust, antecedently to any positive command or prohibition of God; but that the arbitrary will and pleasure of God...by its commands and prohibitions, is the first and only rule and measure thereof. Whence it follows unavoidably, that nothing can be imagined so grossly wicked, or so foully unjust or dishonest, but if it were supposed to be commanded by this omnipotent Deity, must needs upon that hypothesis forthwith become holy, just, and righteous.[24]

Cudworth's point seems to be that if the Control Thesis were true, then anything could be "holy, just, and righteous" – which seems absurd. The problematic implication of the Control Thesis, as Cudworth sees it, is the *contingency* of certain ethical truths. The Control Thesis allegedly implies, for instance, that it could be morally permissible for one person gratuitously to pummel another.

A popular strategy for responding to this kind of objection is to maintain that because it is part of God's essential nature to have a certain type of character (say, to be loving), there are some things such that making them good or right is incompatible with God's essential nature. For example, Edward Wierenga (1983) suggests that because God is all-loving, "He would not command an action which, were it to be performed, would be a gratuitous pummeling of another human being."[25] In this way, it is denied that God could make just any logically consistent ethical claim true. There are some logically consistent ethical claims – for instance that it would be obligatory for someone to inflict a gratuitous pummeling on another human being – that God cannot make true because doing so is inconsistent with His essential nature. Nevertheless, all true ethical claims are true in virtue of some act of will on the part of God. It is still divine *willing* that determines which ethical claims are true, but the scope of divine willing is limited by the divine character. According to this proposal, the Control Thesis is false because it is incompatible with the claim that God essentially has a character of a certain sort, but the Dependency Thesis is nevertheless true.

I think the revised proposal is unacceptable for two reasons. First, implicit in the proposal is the notion that God has the *power* to make any logically consistent ethical claim true; it is only His character that prevents Him from being able to exercise this power. This implies that if, *per impossibile*, God were not loving, He could make it the case that it is obligatory for someone to inflict a gratuitous pummeling on another human being.[26] But I think that the story about the good competitor – evil competitor contest from Section 2.2 shows that even this more modest claim is false. The point of that story is not merely that there are some ethical truths that no being is *capable of* making true but also that there are some ethical claims that no being is *powerful enough* to make true.[27]

Second, notice that the Dependency Thesis implies that nothing distinct from God is intrinsically good or evil. The claim that the Dependency Thesis is necessarily true implies that it is *impossible* for anything distinct from God to be intrinsically good or evil. This is because intrinsic value is the value a thing has in virtue of its intrinsic nature.[28] If an act of will on the part of God bestows value on something distinct from God, that value cannot be intrinsic. It will be value that the thing has in virtue of something distinct from itself.

I think this implication is problematic for the simple reason that some things distinct from God actually are intrinsically good and some things actually are intrinsically evil. Pain, for example, seems to be an intrinsic evil. It is evil in and of itself; its badness is part of its intrinsic nature and is not bestowed upon it from some external source. Yet the theist who accepts the Dependency Thesis must reject this, and maintain instead that pain is bad only because God made it so.[29]

It may be replied that in making this claim I am begging the question against someone who holds the Dependency Thesis. Do I have an *argument* for my claim that some things are intrinsically good or evil? In response to this charge I appeal to some remarks Roderick Chisholm (1973) makes in *The Problem of the Criterion*. Chisholm's topic in that book is epistemology, and he suggests that if we must choose whether to accept some philosophical principle about knowledge or to accept some obvious truth such as that I know I have hands, we should accept the obvious truth.[30] Similarly, it seems to me that if we must choose between the Dependency Thesis and the claim that pain is intrinsically evil or that falling in love is intrinsically good, it is the Dependency Thesis that should go. An epistemology that leads to the conclusion that individuals cannot know they have hands should be rejected; similarly, a metaphysics that leads to the conclusion that falling in love is not intrinsically good, or that pain is not intrinsically evil, should be rejected. In this vein Nielsen writes:

> God or no God, the torturing of innocents is vile. More generally, even if we can make nothing of the concept of God, we can readily come to appreciate . . . that, if anything is evil, inflicting or tolerating unnecessary and pointless suffering is evil, especially when something can be done about it. . . . Can't we be more confident about this than we can about any abstract or general philosophical point we might make in ethical theory?[31]

I conclude, therefore, that the Dependency Thesis should be rejected along with the Control Thesis. If this is correct, then the God as the source of ethics argument, because it is based on the claim that the Dependency Thesis is necessarily true, fails.[32]

2.4 AN ALTERNATIVE ACCOUNT

Rejecting these two theses raises some questions. If the Dependency Thesis is false, then there are some true ethical claims whose truth is not due to some act of will on the part of God. What, then, makes these ethical claims true? If the Control Thesis is false, then there are some logically consistent ethical claims that not even God could make true. Why is God unable to make such claims true? Is this inability consistent with God's omnipotence?

One view that provides answers to these questions is the view that *some ethical truths are necessary truths.*[33] Consider, for instance, the claim that suffering is intrinsically evil. I suggest that this ethical claim is true, and, furthermore, that it is a necessary truth. This claim is true not just in the actual world but in every possible world. Just as there is no possible universe in which $2 + 2 = 5$, there is no possible universe in which suffering is not intrinsically evil. Suffering is bad in virtue of its intrinsic nature – and this is true in every possible universe.

This is a view that can be accepted by atheist and theist alike. With respect to the question, what makes these ethical claims true? my answer is that it is the same sort of thing that makes other necessary truths true – namely, the essential nature of the entities that those claims are about. It is the essential character of the numbers 2 and 5, and of the relations addition and identity, that make it the case that necessarily, $2 + 2$ is not equal to 5. It is the essential nature of pain that makes it the case that it is intrinsically evil. This view also explains why God is unable to render such claims false and how this is compatible with His omnipotence. He is unable to render them false because they simply cannot be rendered false; as necessary truths, they have but one possible truth value – true. It is widely held that omnipotence does not include the ability to do what is impossible. Making necessary falsehoods true is impossible. Thus the fact that God cannot make baby-torture for the sake of entertainment morally permissible does not imply that He is not omnipotent.

I do not mean to suggest that all ethical truths are necessarily true. Indeed, it is clear that many ethical truths are contingent truths. For instance, suppose that I promise to meet you for lunch on a certain occasion. Also suppose that on the occasion in question I have no sufficiently weighty reason not to keep my promise. It follows that I am obligated to meet you for lunch. This is an ethical truth, yet it is a contingent truth. I might not have promised to meet you in the first place; indeed, I might not have been born at all. In either case, the ethical claim in question would have been false. But it seems to me that contingent ethical truths like these are always partly grounded in some necessary ethical truth (or truths). In this case, the relevant truth is something like, "It is morally wrong to fail to keep a promise unless you have some sufficiently weighty reason for doing so."[34]

These necessary ethical truths, I believe, are part of the furniture of the universe. If God exists, they are not rendered true by Him nor are they dependent upon His will for their truth. Moreover, at least some of them are such that He lacks the power to render them false. These necessary ethical truths constitute the ethical background of every possible universe. It is within this framework that all beings and their actions, divine and human alike, are to be evaluated.

Still, it is consistent with this view that God, if He exists, has some role in shaping the moral system to which human beings are subject. That this is so may be seen by considering a familiar kind of case involving humans. Suppose a friend of yours does a huge favor for you. He is happy to do you the favor, but notes (correctly) that "you owe me one." A few weeks later, we may suppose, your friend calls you and informs you that he really needs to borrow your car for the day. You have no pressing need for the car yourself and your friend gently reminds you of the favor he did for you. It is plausible to suppose that, under these circumstances, you have a moral obligation to loan your friend your car for the day.[35] In this case, your friend's request to borrow the car has imposed an obligation on you that you would not otherwise have had. Moreover, there are a variety of obligations your friend could have imposed on you other than the obligation to loan him your car, as there are plenty of other reasonable requests he might have made instead. But of course your friend is not an all-powerful arbiter of morality. It is precisely the framework of necessary ethical truth that enables your friend to impose the obligation in question upon you. The system of morality itself licenses this sort of thing under certain circumstances. This case suggests another possible relationship between God and ethics. This type of relationship is the topic of the next section.

2.5 GOD AS DIVINE COMMANDER

We often find ourselves faced with certain obligations because of how we are related to others. When someone is my friend or spouse, I have obligations to that other person that I would not otherwise have. For example, if I am married to X, then I am morally obligated to be faithful toward X in a way that I would not be if I were not married to X. Some of these relationships seem to be essential to the human condition. For instance, every human being has two genetic parents.[36] This feature of the human condition imposes obligations on humans that they would not otherwise have; arguably, we have obligations toward our parents that we do not have toward any other human being. Imagine for a moment that a theory of spontaneous generation of humans is correct – that is, that rather than being born, human beings have no parents and instead simply grow spontaneously out of the ground from time to time. In a world like that, no human being would be genetically related to any other human being, and the obligations of humans in such a world would be quite different from the obligations of humans in our world. This suggests that whether or not human beings have a *divine creator* may affect the moral obligations that human beings have. If God did exist, then perhaps we would have moral obligations that we in fact do not have (supposing that naturalism is true).[37] It is important to distinguish two claims here. The first is the modest claim that the existence of God brings with it *some* moral obligations that we would not have if God did not exist. The other claim is the so-called "Karamazov's Thesis."[38] This is the thesis that if God does not exist, then all human actions are morally permissible and human beings have no moral obligations at all. Without God, anything goes.

Why might someone accept Karamazov's Thesis? One answer to this question has its roots in the Platonic (1977) dialogue *Phaedo*. In that dialogue, Socrates says that "the gods are our guardians and that men are one of their possessions."[39] Some Biblical passages indicate the presence of this strand of thought in the Judeo-Christian tradition as well. In the Old Testament, God sometimes refers to the Israelites as His "treasured possession."[40] Picking up on this idea, Baruch Brody (1974) makes the following tentative suggestion:

> [I]f we are the property of God, then perhaps we just have an obliga-
> tion to do whatever he says, and then perhaps we can . . . consider the
> possible claim that . . . actions are right (wrong) for us to do just in case
> and only because God, who has created and owns us and whom we
> therefore have an obligation to follow, wants us to do (refrain from
> doing) them.[41]

Brody's "possible claim" is, strictly speaking, incompatible with Karamazov's Thesis because the right-hand side of Brody's bi-conditional is false if God does not exist.[42] According to Brody's principle, if God does not exist then nothing is morally wrong – but nothing is morally right either. Still, Brody's principle implies that without God, human beings have no moral obligations – and that is the claim in which we are most interested.

Brody considers the objection that owning a human being is "an unjust act, one that cannot meaningfully be ascribed to an all just being."[43] As Brody sees it, the crucial question is, "is it unjust for God, who is vastly superior to us and is our creator, to possess human beings?"[44] But let us suppose that it is just for God to possess human beings, and that if God exists all humans are His property. It seems to me that it does not follow from this that without God, human beings have no moral obligations. This is because the claim that (1) Being X owns Being Y does not imply (2) the *only* moral obligations Y has are the ones imposed by X. Such an inference is open to a variety of counterexamples; I will present just one. Suppose that X and Y are married to each other and both are the property of Z. Under these circumstances, X and Y will have a variety of obligations. Some of these obligations may derive from Z's ownership of X and Y – but others will derive from the marriage relation that obtains between X and Y themselves. If X and Y were not owned by Z, they might have fewer obligations than they do have – but they would still have some obligations. Specifically, they would still have the various obligations that arise from the fact that they are married to each other. So the claim that human beings are God's property does not establish Karamazov's Thesis.

There are grounds for maintaining that God has the authority to impose moral obligations on us other than the claim that we are God's property. Brody considers the idea that "we have an obligation to follow God's wishes because he is our creator."[45] Brody's suggestion is that even if we are not God's property, the fact that He is our creator may put Him in a position to impose various moral obligations upon us. Recall the example of your friend who was in a position to impose certain moral obligations upon you because you "owed him one." If God did exist, perhaps we, too, would "owe Him one" for creating us, and consequently He would be in a position to impose obligations upon us.

Adams examines the idea that the gratitude we owe to God might license Him to impose obligations upon us. Among the reasons humans might have to obey God, Adams includes "reasons of gratitude," such as the facts that "God is our creator ... God loves us ... God gives us all the goods we enjoy ... [the] covenants God has made with us for our good ... or other things God has done to save us or bring us to the greatest good."[46] Similarly, in his book *The God Who Commands*, Richard Mouw (1996) writes:

> The God who issues the "Thou shalts" of Exodus 20 is the one who prefaces those directives with the reminder that we have been delivered from the house of bondage. And the one who, in the New Testament, tells us to keep his commandments, does so on the basis of the fact that when we were yet sinners he died for us. The God who commands in the Scriptures is the one who offers the broken chariots of the Egpytians and the nail-scarred hands of the divine Son as a vindication of the right to tell us what to do.[47]

A second possible basis for God's status as our rightful commander has to do not with the gratitude we owe God but rather with God's intrinsic nature:

> God is supremely knowledgeable and wise.... God is the Good itself,
> supremely beautiful and rich in nonmoral as well as moral perfec-
> tion.... One important excellence is justice. It clearly matters to the
> persuasive power of God's character, as a source of moral obligation,
> that the divine will is just.[48]

Adams also points to the goodness of God's commands themselves,
declaring that, "[I]t is crucial...that the behavior that God commands is not bad, but good, either intrinsically or by serving a pattern of life that is very good."[49] Still another ground is suggested by
Swinburne:

> God is the creator of the inanimate world and, not being known to
> have ceded ownership of it, is properly judged its owner.... The owner
> of property has the right to tell those to whom he has loaned it what
> they are allowed to do with it. Consequently God has a right to lay
> down how that property, the inanimate world, shall be used and by
> whom. If God has made the Earth, he can say which of his children
> can use which part.[50]

There are, then, a wide range of plausible reasons for the idea that
if God did exist, He would be authorized to impose certain moral
obligations on human beings.[51] It is important to notice that the sort
of view suggested by Adams and the others is quite different from
the view that in virtue of His omnipotence, God has the power of
constructing ethics through the force of His will. The view under
consideration now is that in virtue of some *ethical* feature or features
of God (such as His goodness) or some ethically significant relationship between humans and God (He is our creator, or our savior), God
is authorized to impose moral obligations upon us. According to this
sort of view, God is our duly authorized commander. Though both
kinds of view reasonably may be labeled 'divine command theories,'
they differ from each other in significant ways. I have already argued
that the first sort of view is false. Now I will argue not that the second
sort of view is false, but rather that it is inconsistent with Karamazov's
Thesis and hence hardly can be used to establish that thesis.[52] The
second type of divine command theory can be used legitimately to
establish that if God exists, then *some* of our moral obligations are imposed on us by God. But it cannot be used to establish the stronger

conclusion that if God exists, then *all* of our moral obligations are imposed on us by God.

My argument turns on the following question: *How* exactly could God impose obligations on human beings? That is, suppose that God is our duly authorized commander. Through what *process* could God impose obligations on us? This question does not seem to arise on the previously discussed view that God is the omnipotent creator of ethical truth. On that view, God renders certain ethical claims true in much the same way that He renders certain physical claims true – by simply willing that they be true. But a duly authorized commander cannot impose moral obligations *merely* by willing them into existence. So if we are thinking of God according to this model, we must inquire into the nature of the process by which God imposes obligations upon us. In his paper "Divine Command, Divine Will, and Moral Obligation" Mark Murphy (1998) usefully outlines the three main options, which are that God can impose on person S the moral obligation to do A: (1) by *commanding* S to do A; (2) by *willing that S be morally obligated* to do A; or (3) by *willing* that S do A.[53]

Let us consider the three possibilities in reverse order. One of the main problems facing a proponent of option (3) is that of specifying the appropriate sense of 'willing' as it appears in (3):

> The difficulty that lurks in specifying such a sense is this. If one specifies a sense of willing that is too strong, it would follow that no one could possibly violate a moral requirement; if one specifies a sense of willing that is too weak, it does not seem appropriate to connect that sense to moral obligation; and it is not easy to specify a sense of willing that falls between these unacceptable extremes.[54]

Murphy takes a shot at specifying the appropriate sense by borrowing Aquinas's distinction between antecedent and consequent willing:

> What Aquinas calls consequent willing is what God in fact wills. . . . Antecedent willing is, on the other hand, a relative abstraction, for we do not 'will simply, what we will antecedently.' Thus, Aquinas holds that antecedently God wills that all humans be saved, but He does not will this consequently.[55]

The distinction might be explained best by way of a simple example. Suppose you are like I am and enjoy a nice slice of cheesecake from time to time. You might antecedently will to eat a piece of cheesecake if one is available. However, finding yourself in a situation in which you know the available piece of cheesecake to be poisoned, you will consequently to refrain from eating it.

Murphy explains how God's antecedent willings determine the moral obligations of human beings in these lines:

> Antecedent intentions are . . . relative abstractions; and since there are various levels of abstraction to which we can ascend in the ascription of such intentions, there will be a variety of antecedent intentions. We may characterize one's *ultima facie* [all–in] moral obligations . . . as depending on God's antecedent intentions concerning one's actions which take into account all circumstances of action apart from what one actually chooses to do.[56]

If you are in fact going to torture an innocent baby on Sunday afternoon just for fun, then God knows this and so will not will consequently that you refrain from torturing the baby. But His most specific antecedent willing – the one that takes into account every detail of the situation except the fact that you are going to torture the baby – is that you refrain from torturing the baby. On Murphy's account, this makes it the case that you have an obligation to refrain from torturing the baby.

Adams suggests that this type of view fails because of the possibility of cases in which "God wants us to do something but does not command us to do it."[57] Adams elaborates on this point as follows:

> For many reasons, we often do not want people to be *obliged* to do what we want them to *do*. So far as I can see, God can have such reasons too, so that we should not expect God to want God's wanting someone to do something to impose, automatically, an obligation to do it.[58]

The point here is that option (3) implies that it is impossible for God merely to want a person to perform a certain action without that person being morally obligated to perform the action. According to (3), the willing itself imposes the obligation. A possible case of the sort

Adams has in mind occurs in Milton's *Paradise Lost*. After the creation of Adam but prior to the creation of Eve, Adam asks God to create an equal companion for him. Initially God resists, first suggesting that Adam's complaint that he is lonely is unwarranted, declaring "What call'st thou solitude? Is not the earth / With various living creatures and the air / Replenish'd, and all these at thy command / To come and play before thee?"[59] Adam persists, and God next points out that He, despite lacking an equal companion, is perfectly happy; why, then, should Adam's lack of such a companion prevent him from being happy?[60] Adam replies that God is perfect whereas man is not; hence man's need for an equal companion. Finally, God relents:

> Thus far to try thee, Adam, I was pleas'd, / And find thee knowing not of beasts alone, / Which thou hast rightly nam'd, but of thy self, / Expressing well the spirit within thee free, / My image, not imparted to the brute; / Whose fellowship therefore, unmeet for thee, / Good reason was thou freely should'st dislike. / And be so minded still: I, ere thou spak'st, / Knew it not good for man to be alone, / And no such company as then thou saw'st / Intended thee, for trial only brought, / To see how thou could'st judge of fit and meet.[61]

It turns out that God wanted Adam to have an equal companion all along – and He wanted Adam to recognize his need for such a companion on his own and to ask God to create a companion for him. But it seems implausible to suppose that in wanting this, God thereby imposed on Adam the moral obligation to ask God for a companion. It is surely possible that God wanted Adam to ask for a companion without Adam being obligated to make the request. One problem with option (3), then, is that it actually seems to impose unacceptable restrictions on what God can do.

Another difficulty with (3) may be seen by recalling the case of the friend to whom you owe the favor. It seems absurd to suppose that your friend could impose on you the obligation to loan him your car merely by *willing* that you do so! If he fails to communicate his will to you in some fashion, no obligation is imposed upon you. But the same thing would seem to be true with respect to God. From the fact that God has the authority to impose obligations on human beings it does not follow that He can impose obligations merely by willing that people perform certain actions. As Adams puts it: "Games in which one party incurs guilt for failing to guess the unexpressed wishes of the other party are not nice games. They are no nicer if God is thought of as a party to them."[62]

This latter point tells against option (2) as well. Option (2) implies that God, our duly authorized commander, can impose moral obligations on us merely by willing that we have certain moral obligations but without communicating to us what these obligations might be. Again, this seems implausible; your friend may want you to be obligated to loan him your car, but no such obligation exists until he actually makes the request.

These considerations suggest that option (1) is the most plausible option of the three. I will argue, however, that if the only way God can impose moral obligations on human beings is by commanding them to perform certain actions, there will be limits to the obligations God can impose – and the nature of these limits will provide a reason for rejecting the view that God could be the source of *all* of our moral obligations.

Adams favors option (1), and he points out that to evaluate it, something must be said about what it is for God to issue a command to a human being. Adams specifies three conditions that must be met:

> (1) A divine command will always involve a *sign*, as we may call it, that is intentionally caused by God. (2) In causing the sign God must intend to issue a command, and *what* is commanded is what God intends to command thereby. (3) The sign must be such that the intended audience could understand it as conveying the intended command.[63]

It is not clear if Adams intends these three conditions to be jointly sufficient for God to impose a moral obligation on human beings by way of a divine command. If he does, though, then I think Adams has left out an important condition. Recall the example of the friend to whom you owe a favor. Suppose your friend (call him "Dave") sends you an anonymous note. The note reads: "Loan Dave your car." In this case, your friend has given you a sign that he intentionally caused and, in so doing, intends to issue to you the command to loan him your car. Moreover, you are clearly capable of understanding the note as conveying the command to you to loan Dave your car. Are you now morally obligated to loan Dave your car? The answer clearly enough is no, and it is not hard to see why: You have no idea who issued this command. More specifically, you don't know that the command was issued by Dave. Moreover, Dave (we may reasonably suppose) knew that you would not be able to tell who issued the command. In these circumstances, it seems clear that Dave, despite being capable of imposing on you the obligation to loan him your car, has failed to do so in the case at hand. He has failed to do so because he has failed to get you to recognize that the command is coming from a legitimate source.

In his discussion of God's credentials as a moral commander, Mouw emphasizes the importance of recognizing that the commands one receives have a legitimate source:

> Whether a given individual possesses the authority to command our obedience is a matter which must be decided by examining the credentials of the would-be commander.... [We should be] sensitive to the need to examine the credentials of others who claim the authority to be moral commanders.[64]

If God is to impose moral obligations on humans by way of His divine commands, He must get his intended audience to recognize that the commands are coming from Him. The case of Dave illustrates that it is not enough merely for God to have the right credentials; those whom He would command must *recognize* that the commands in question are coming from an appropriately credentialed God. But it seems clear that there are plenty of people who do not believe that God has issued any commands to anyone – naturalists, for example. A naturalist denies the existence of supernatural beings of any sort. Furthermore, a naturalist does not believe that there is someone who created us, or made the relevant covenants with us, or died for our sins, or is omniscient and perfectly good.

We may distinguish two kinds of naturalist. The first is a *reasonable naturalist*. A reasonable naturalist holds an epistemic position such that it is reasonable to withhold belief in God. The second is an *unrea-sonable naturalist*, whose epistemic position makes it *not* reasonable to withhold belief in God.

It seems clear that God has not imposed any obligations on rea-sonable naturalists by way of divine commands.[65] A reasonable nat-uralist does not believe that any command has God as its source. Moreover, it is logical for a reasonable naturalist to withhold belief that a given command is a divine command. It might be thought that any divine command would *obviously* have God as its source. But if this were true, and if divine commands had been issued to everyone, then the existence of God would be *obvious* to everyone – which it plainly is not. Moreover, some of the things that Adams counts as divine commands do not obviously have God as their source:

> Principles of moral obligation constituted by divine commands are not timeless truths, because the commands are given by signs that occur in time. People who are not in the region of space–time in which a sign can be known are not subject to a command given by it. Of course, if the signs by which some divine commands are given are moral impulses and sensibilities common to practically all adult human beings since some (not too recent) point in the evolution of our species, all of us can fairly be counted as subject to those commands.[66]

Here Adams suggests that "moral impulses and sensibilities" can be the signs by which God issues divine commands. But these are hardly signs whose divine origin is obvious; they seem fairly akin to anony-mous notes.

If God does not impose moral obligations on reasonable naturalists by way of divine commands, it follows either that (1) reasonable nat-uralists have no moral obligations, or (2) some humans have moral obligations that are not derived from divine commands. Option (1) is implausible and something no theist would want to accept. Surely the theist will not allow that the naturalist, in virtue of his natural-ism, is allowed to do whatever he wants! It seems, therefore, that we must conclude that there are some moral obligations that are not derived from divine commands. God as the divine commander is not the source of all of our moral obligations; even the theist ought to admit that at least some obligations have some other basis.

It might be objected that all naturalists are unreasonable naturalists. Even if this dubious claim is true, it still follows that there are moral obligations that are not derived from divine commands. Consider once more the example of you and Dave. Suppose that Dave knows that you are unreasonable in the following way: You refuse to believe of anyone who calls you on the telephone that he is who he says he is. Knowing this, Dave cannot impose a moral obligation on you by way of a command issued over the phone, because he knows that you will (unreasonably) fail to recognize that the command is coming from him. Similarly, God cannot impose moral obligations on unreasonable naturalists by way of divine commands because they will (unreasonably, we may suppose) fail to recognize that such commands are coming from God. There are two points worth making here. First, this case is to be carefully distinguished from the case of a person who does recognize that a given command is coming from God but who refuses to admit this. This is not the case of the unreasonable naturalist, who genuinely fails to recognize a divine source for any command. Second, the claim here is not that an unreasonable naturalist is entirely above criticism. Suppose that God issues a command to a certain unreasonable naturalist to perform action A. The unreasonable naturalist, failing to recognize God as the source of this command, fails to perform action A. The unreasonable naturalist may be open to criticism: Failure to recognize that the command has a divine source may be *irrational*.[67] Nevertheless, God has failed to impose on the unreasonable naturalist the moral obligation *to perform action A*, and so we cannot say that something morally wrong was done in failing to perform action A (unless of course there was already an obligation to perform A for some other reason). Returning to the case of Dave, you can be criticized for unreasonably failing to believe that it is Dave on the other end of the line, but it cannot be said that you have violated a moral obligation in failing to loan Dave your car. Dave failed to impose that moral obligation on you because you failed to recognize his command to loan him your car as coming from him.

We can conclude, therefore, that the presence of naturalists in the world – whether they are reasonable or unreasonable – teaches us that there are some moral obligations that are not derived from divine commands. God may impose *some* moral obligations on human beings by way of His divine commands, but not all of our moral obligations are so imposed.

What might be the basis of obligations that are not divinely imposed? I have already suggested that some of our moral obligations derive from the various relationships we have to other human beings. But I do not think that all of our obligations derive from such relationships. Obligations may also be grounded in intrinsic value. A very strong version of this view is proposed by Moore, who maintains that "the assertion 'I am morally bound to perform this action' is identical with the assertion 'This action will produce the greatest possible amount of good in the Universe.'"[68] One need not be a thoroughgoing consequentialist of the Moorean variety, though, to recognize the truth of claims like this one: If I know that I can prevent some intrinsic evil without thereby introducing a greater evil into the world – or sacrificing some good, or violating some obligation, or doing anything else morally untoward – then I have a moral obligation to prevent the evil in question. If I can prevent an innocent baby from being tortured merely by lifting my finger (and doing so will have no morally untoward consequences) then I have a moral obligation to prevent the baby from being tortured. This obligation does not derive from any relationship between the baby and myself, or from any relationship between myself or the baby and some third party. Rather, it derives from the fact that an innocent baby being tortured is a fantastically bad thing. This is an obligation I have regardless of whether I stand in any interesting relationship to any other being – including a divine creator.

These points allow us to respond to some rhetorical questions posed by Craig (1996): "If God does not exist, then it is difficult to see any reason to think that human beings are special or that their morality is objectively true. Moreover, why think that we have any moral obligations to do anything? Who or what imposes any moral duties upon us?"[69]

The proper response to Craig's first rhetorical question is that we have some moral obligations that derive from our relationships with other human beings and we have other moral obligations that derive from intrinsic values. The proper response to Craig's second question is that many of our moral duties are such that no being *imposes* them upon us. Craig's mistake is in thinking that the set of moral obligations we have is coextensive with the set of moral obligations that are imposed on us by some being. The truth is that even if God exists, the latter is a proper subset of the former.

It appears, then, that the idea that if God does not exist everything is permissible is an overreaction. Consider the case of a man who, having extricated himself from an increasingly unhappy romantic relationship, thinks, "I'm free! I can do whatever I want!" Of course if taken literally this claim is false, but most likely what he means is that it is morally permissible for him to do all sorts of things that it was not permissible for him to do while he was in the relationship. Breaking up with his girlfriend has not made it permissible for him to torture babies for fun. Similarly, if modern man has discovered that God does not exist, he has not thereby also discovered that it is permissible for him to do anything he wants. Instead, he has merely discovered that it is permissible from him to do some things that he previously believed were not permissible for him to do. He has discovered, for instance, that he has much more latitude, morally speaking, in how he spends his Sundays. He has not discovered, though, that it is permissible for him to devote his Sunday afternoons to the torture of helpless infants.

There is, of course, much more to be said about the basis of the moral obligations we have that are not imposed on us by God. My goal here, however, is not to develop a complete atheistic meta-ethical theory.[70] My goal instead has been to show that the idea that God is the complete source of all ethical truths, or even of all our moral obligations, leads to problematic consequences and hence should be rejected.

I have yet to encounter a discussion of the relationship between God and ethics that does not at least allude to the Platonic (1948) dialogue *Euthyphro*. I have no wish to break with tradition, so let us briefly consider that dialogue. The dialogue begins with Socrates encountering Euthyphro in the Hall of the King. Socrates is there to defend himself against the charges of Meletus, which initiate the trial that will eventually lead to Socrates' execution. Euthyphro is there because he intends to prosecute his father for the murder of one of the family's laborers. The laborer had killed one of the family's slaves in a drunken rage, and Euthyphro's father tied up the laborer and threw him in a ditch while trying to decide what to do with him. The laborer subsequently died of cold and hunger. Euthyphro notes that his family objects to what he is doing and makes the following remark: "They assert . . . that I ought not to concern myself about such a person because it is impious for a son to prosecute his father for murder. So little, Socrates, do they know the divine law of piety and impiety."[71]

As a consequence of his claim that he knows a thing or two about the nature of piety, Euthyphro soon finds himself embroiled in a complicated philosophical discussion with Socrates. In the midst of this discussion Socrates poses what has become one of the most discussed of all the questions Plato ever put into Socrates' mouth: "Do the gods love piety because it is pious, or is it pious because they love it?"[72] This question is the basis of the so-called "Euthyphro Dilemma."

The answer I have proposed to this kind of question is that if God exists, some actions may be obligatory because God has commanded us to do them. But not all actions are like this. Moreover, at least some good things are not good because God loves them. Instead, some things are intrinsically good. An unqualified endorsement of the second horn of the dilemma Socrates poses is not a reasonable position. The foundation of morality is a set of axiomatic necessary ethical truths. No being, natural or supernatural, is responsible for the truth of or has control over these ethical truths.[73]

The view I have outlined, then, is inconsistent with the idea that all ethical truth is a function of human decisions and/or conventions, as well as the idea that all ethical truth is a function of divine activity. Each of these two views has its adherents. Why might this be? One possibility is a narrow focus on examples of a certain kind. Some ethical truths do depend, at least in part, on human conventions. Consider, for instance, the moral obligation each of us has to drive on the right-hand side of the road (in two-way traffic) in the United States. An exclusive focus on this sort of example may lead one to the mistaken conclusion that *all* ethical truths depend on human conventions. If God exists, then some ethical truths may depend, at least in part, on divine activity. Consider for instance the moral obligation that some theists allegedly have to refrain from idol worship.[74] An exclusive focus on this sort of example may lead one to the mistaken conclusion that *all* ethical truths depend on divine activity. Both of these views are wrong, though. In each case, the dependency in question is grounded in a more fundamental ethical truth. With respect to the first example, each of us has at least a *prima facie* moral obligation to obey the relevant traffic laws. With respect to the second example, we have already considered a variety of reasons humans might have for obeying God's commands. For example, it may be that each of us has a *prima facie* moral obligation to obey a God who died for our sins.

I would like to conclude this chapter with a brief consideration of a bold conjecture made by John Leslie (1989) in his book *Universes*:

> The reason why there exists something rather than nothing could be as follows: that *ethical needs for the existence of things are in some cases creatively effective.* . . . God may be an all-powerful person, an omniscient Designer who owes his existence, knowledge, and power to the fact that these are ethically required.[75]

Leslie presents an interesting twist on the Euthyphro dilemma: Not only is it not the case that God's love for things makes those things good; it is Goodness itself that has brought God into existence. Leslie's suggestion, in brief, is that a personal God exists because it is ethically required that such a being exists. While I do not accept this view, I think that Leslie has the order of priority between a personal God and ethical truth right. If there are ethical truths at all, then some of them lie at the very bedrock of reality, created by no one, under no one's control, passing judgment on the actions and character of God and man alike.[76]

THREE

THE DIVINE GUARANTEE
OF PERFECT JUSTICE

"[O]ne is never just willingly but only when compelled to be. No one believes justice to be a good when it is kept private, since, wherever either person thinks he can do injustice with impunity, he does it. Indeed, every man believes that injustice is far more profitable to himself than justice."

–Glaucon[1]

3.1 WHY BE MORAL?

Suppose that, as I have argued, human beings have various moral obligations even if God does not exist. Some theists might grant this but allege that if God does not exist, then we have *no reason to care* about such obligations. In a Godless universe certain actions may be morally obligatory and others may be morally wrong, but there is no reason for human beings to be particularly interested in which are which. We may turn once again to William Craig for a suggestion along these lines:

Even if there were objective moral values and duties under naturalism, they are irrelevant because there is no moral accountability. If life ends at the grave, it makes no difference whether one lives as a Stalin or as a saint.... Why should you sacrifice your self-interest and especially your life for the sake of someone else? There can be no good reason for adopting such a self-negating course of action on the naturalistic world view.... Life is too short to jeopardize it by acting out of anything but pure self–interest. Sacrifice for another person is just stupid.[2]

Simon Blackburn (1998) has observed that the statement 'X has a reason to A' can be understood as "a descriptive remark about X's psychology, or a normative remark about what X ought to be responsive to, whether or not she is."[3] Let us call a reason in the first sense a *psychological reason* and a reason in the latter sense a *normative reason*.[4] Suppose that I am aware that the slice of cheesecake before me is laced with arsenic but don't much care. I have no inclination to refrain from eating the cheesecake. In this case we may say that while I have no psychological reason to refrain from eating the cheesecake (I am not in fact motivated to refrain from eating it), I have a normative reason to refrain from doing so (I *should* be motivated to refrain from eating it). That the cheesecake is poisoned constitutes a (normative) reason for me to refrain from eating the cheesecake – a reason to which I am indifferent.

Craig clearly intends to be discussing normative reasons. His claim is not that if God does not exist, then no one is in fact motivated to do the right thing. His claim is that if God does not exist, then no one has a normative reason to do the right thing. Only if God exists are we being indifferent toward considerations that ought to concern us by failing to care about where our moral duty lies.[5]

Craig's claim is related to one of the most ancient challenges in Western ethical philosophy. Plato puts the challenge into the mouth of Glaucon in the *Republic* in the epigraph for this chapter. The challenge is often posed in the form of a question: Why should we be moral? It can also be posed in the form of an argument. Although there are countless ways of posing the challenge, it will be most useful for our purposes here to consider a very general version of the challenge. The challenge will be taken as an attack on the claim that any human being ever has a normative reason to be moral. Being moral will be understood broadly, so that fulfilling one's moral obligations, inculcating virtuous character in oneself, performing virtuous actions, and acting in a supererogatory fashion all count as ways of being moral. With this in mind, the challenge can be formulated this way:

The Moral Challenge

1. A person has a normative reason to be moral only if it is in that person's best interest to be moral.
2. It is never in anyone's best interest to be moral.
3. Therefore, no one ever has a normative reason to be moral.[6]

3.2 FIRST ANSWER: BECAUSE MORALITY AND SELF-INTEREST COINCIDE

One popular strategy for responding to this challenge is to attack the second premise. If it can be shown that it is always, or at least generally or even often in a person's interest to be moral – that morality and self-interest always or often coincide – then the question "why should we be moral?" can be given an adequate answer. This kind of strategy is pursued, in different ways, by a number of prominent Western philosophers, including Plato, Aristotle, and Hume.[7]

The theist can also make use of this kind of strategy. The key element of the theistic response to the challenge is the concept of an afterlife in which the moral are rewarded and the immoral are punished. If God exists, then there is a divine guarantee of perfect justice; in the end, all the individuals who ever lived will receive precisely the fate they deserve. If God exists, then there is a perfect correlation between morality and self-interest. Craig explains it this way:

> [O]n the theistic hypothesis God holds all persons morally accountable for their actions. Evil and wrong will be punished; righteousness will be vindicated. Good ultimately triumphs over evil, and we shall finally see that we do live in a moral universe after all. Despite the inequities of this life, in the end the scales of God's justice will be balanced. Thus, the moral choices we make in this life are infused with an eternal significance.[8]

It is important to distinguish two claims here. The first is the claim that if God does not exist, then we have *no* reason to be moral. The second is the claim that if God does exist, then we have a reason to be moral that we lack if God does not exist – namely, the divine guarantee of justice. While the second claim may be true, I believe that the first claim is false. Before explaining why it is false, it will be useful to consider some nontheistic ways of rejecting the second premise of the moral challenge. Doing so will be instructive because it will reveal just how much philosophical work would be required of a theist like Craig, who maintains that the theistic response is the only adequate way of dealing with the challenge. Such a theist would need to show that the nontheistic responses are unsuccessful – and this is something that Craig, at least, has not even attempted to do.

For our first nontheistic attack on the second premise of the moral challenge we may turn once again to that Stagiran giant, Aristotle. As I noted in Chapter 1, Aristotle singles out contemplation as the intrinsically best sort of activity. But he also maintains that ethically virtuous activity is intrinsically good, although not as good as theoretical contemplation. The best possible kind of human life is one filled with theoretical contemplation; a life filled with ethically virtuous activity is also a good human life, although not as good as the life of the philosopher.[9] On Aristotle's view, then, virtuous activity is its own reward. Aristotle appeals to this idea to explain why an ethically virtuous person is willing to engage in actions that might be viewed as acts of self-sacrifice:

> [M]any actions of a [virtuous person] are performed in the interest of his friends and of his country, and if there be need, he will give his life for them. He will freely give his money, honors, and, in short, all good things that men compete for, while he gains nobility of himself.... A good man would freely give away his money if it means that his friend would get more, for (in this way) the friend's gain is wealth, while his own is nobility, so that he assigns the greater good to himself.[10]

A person who generously gives a needy friend some money loses money but "gains" (that is, engages in) generous action – and the generous action is the greater good. To one who values money more than virtuous activity, such an action seems to be an act of self-sacrifice, but, on Aristotle's view, the wise person knows that the giver has gotten the better end of the bargain. It truly is better to give than to receive in the sense that the activity of giving is a greater benefit to the giver than the money received is to the recipient. Aristotle even tries to show that sometimes sacrificing one's life is in one's own best interest:

> [A virtuous person] would rather live nobly for one full year than lead an indifferent existence for many; and he would rather perform one great and noble act than many insignificant ones. People who die for a cause achieve this perhaps, and they clearly choose great nobility for themselves.[11]

Suppose we imagine a graph that depicts the amount of virtuous activity throughout a given person's life, where the x-axis indicates time and the y-axis indicates the level of virtuous activity in which the person is engaged at a given time. One way of understanding the passage I just quoted is that Aristotle is suggesting that the total value of a person's life (for that person) is not simply the area under the curve on the graph in question. Rather, Aristotle may hold a holistic view, according to which a life with one or two large spikes of virtuous activity is a better life than one with a relatively low, stable, and long-lasting level of virtuous activity – *even if the total amount of virtuous activity in the second life is greater than the amount in the first life*. A noble sacrifice of one's own life – while of course putting an end to one's life and hence to all of one's virtuous activity – also produces a huge spike of virtuous activity. This spike may well produce a life that is better for one who lives it than a longer life without that spike. On this view, martyrdom can be the option that maximizes one's own self-interest – even if there is no afterlife and death is the permanent end of conscious experience.[12]

Aristotle responds to the moral challenge by proposing what we might call a *revisionist axiology*. Let us suppose with Aristotle that what most people believe to be most valuable are things like power, wealth, good reputation, and pleasure. We might call the view that these are the best things in life – the goods that make human life worth living – the *commonsense axiology*. Aristotle rejects the commonsense axiology and argues instead that activity of a certain kind – activity that flows from an ethically virtuous character – is better than any of these things.[13] Acquiring ethically virtuous character and engaging

72

in ethically virtuous action is a way to live one of the best kinds of lives available to humans; this is why we should be moral.

A different way of responding to the moral challenge is proposed by the atheistic philosopher David Hume (1998c) in the Conclusion of *An Enquiry Concerning the Principles of Morals*. There, Hume asks the rhetorical question, "[W]hat theory of morals can ever serve any useful purpose, unless it can show, by a particular detail, that all the duties, which it recommends, are also the true interest of each individual?"[14] Hume proceeds to try to meet his own requirement:

> [L]et a man suppose that he has full power of modeling his own disposition, and let him deliberate what appetite or desire he would choose for the foundation of his happiness and enjoyment.... Treating vice with the greatest candour, and making it all possible concessions, we must acknowledge, that there is not, in any instance, the smallest pretext for giving it the preference above virtue, with a view to self-interest....[15]

Hume claims that it is virtuous character that is most likely to enable those who have it to lead lives that are good for them. Like Aristotle, Hume maintains that morality and self-interest generally coincide, not because justice is meted out in the afterlife, but because being moral is beneficial in *this* life. However, Hume reaches this conclusion via a route quite different from Aristotle's. Unlike Aristotle, Hume does not reject the commonsense axiology. Instead, he argues that virtuous character leads to precisely the things valued by ordinary people. For example, on Hume's account a central component of virtuous character is a trait he calls "benevolence" or "humanity," which is concern for the well-being of all humans. Hume praises this trait of character for the pleasure it generates for those who possess it:

> [T]he immediate feeling of benevolence and friendship, humanity and kindness, is sweet, smooth, tender, and agreeable, independent of all fortune and accident.... What other passion is there where we shall find so many advantages united; an agreeable sentiment, a pleasing consciousness, a good reputation?[16]

73

Concern for humanity is commended on similar grounds by John Stuart Mill (1979):

> To those who have neither public nor private affections, the excitements of life are much curtailed, and in any case dwindle in value as the time approaches when all selfish interests must be terminated by death; while those who leave after them objects of personal affection, and especially those who have also cultivated a fellow-feeling with the collective interests of mankind, retain as lively an interest in life on the eve of death as in the vigor of youth and health.[17]

Interest in and concern for the success of a professional sports team can produce excitement and pleasure even after one's own athletic abilities have dwindled or vanished entirely. In a similar fashion, being a fan of humanity can produce pleasure even after one's ability to do much of anything at all has dwindled.[18] For this reason Mill recommends becoming a fan of humanity.

Hume's view, then, is that being virtuous is the best way to attain wealth, power, and pleasure; that is why we should be moral. There is, however, a serious challenge to this position which pertains to the sort of person Hume calls a "sensible knave:"

> [A] sensible knave, in particular incidents, may think, that an act of iniquity or infidelity will make a considerable addition to his fortune, without causing any considerable breach in the social union and confederacy. That *honesty is the best policy*, may be a good general rule; but is liable to many exceptions: And he, it may, perhaps, be thought, conducts himself with most wisdom, who observes the general rule, and takes advantage of all the exceptions.[19]

The sensible knave follows the strategy of being honest and just when doing so is to his advantage, but being dishonest and unjust when he knows he can get away with it and when doing so will be to his advantage. He therefore gets the best of both worlds: Because he cheats when and only when he knows he will not be caught, he has a reputation for virtue, and so acquires all the benefits that arise from such a reputation. In addition to these benefits, he gets the added benefits of cheating when he can get away with it – benefits that a genuinely virtuous person will not receive. Therefore, everything else being equal, the sensible knave fares better than the genuinely virtuous person. Is not sensible knavery, then, rather than genuine virtue, the type of character that is most likely to enable those who have it to lead lives that are good for them? If we had the ability to mold our characters as we saw fit, and we wanted to select for ourselves the type of character that would best promote our own happiness, would not sensible knavery be a better choice than genuine virtuousness?

To this sort of challenge, Aristotle would reply that the sensible knave is in fact a fool who engages in vicious activity in order to obtain money, power, wealth, or honor, thereby making himself worse off overall. Just as virtuous activity is one of the greatest goods, so vicious activity is one of the greatest evils, and by engaging in it the sensible knave renders himself miserable.[20] But Hume cannot avail himself of this response because, unlike Aristotle, he accepts the commonsense axiology.

Hume's own response to the challenge is brief. The main element of his response is found in this passage:

> [W]hile they [sensible knaves] purpose to cheat with moderation and secrecy, a tempting incident occurs, nature is frail, and they give into the snare; whence they can never extricate themselves, without a total loss of reputation, and the forfeiture of all future trust and confidence with mankind.[21]

Hume's claim here is that sensible knavery is *too difficult* a strategy for it to be a reasonable way to achieve happiness. The temptation to cheat even when it is not wise to do so is strong, and those who aim for sensible knavery are apt to fall short and end up as not-so-sensible knaves. It is just too hard to cheat only when you know you won't get caught, and the consequences of getting caught are quite severe. In this way, Hume claims that genuine virtuousness is still the *best bet* when it comes to securing your own happiness. Why be moral? Because doing so gives you the best odds of securing a life that is good for you (though it does not guarantee such a life).

But is Hume right? Is it really so difficult to be a sensible knave? One might wonder whether this is just a piece of wishful thinking. Hume offers no support for the claim. There is, however, a recent book that offers evidence from psychology to support Hume's claim, thereby filling in a serious lacuna in Hume's argument. The book in question is Robert Frank's (1988) *Passions Within Reason*. Frank appeals to what psychologists call "the matching law" to support Hume's rejection of the sensible knave (whom Frank calls the "opportunist"). The matching law states that "the attractiveness of a reward is inversely proportional to its delay."[22] Human beings tend to assign greater importance to temporally closer rewards and punishments than they do to more temporally distant ones.[23] This aspect of human psychology poses a serious problem for the would-be sensible knave:

> The problem is that the material gains from cheating come right away, the penalties only much later. . . . If our psychological reward mechanism really does assign disproportional weight to near–term rewards, a person who cares only about material rewards will cheat even when it is not prudent to do so.

Because of the matching law, Frank suggests, would-be sensible knaves will eventually cheat when it is not wise to do so and will get caught. Because of the way the human mind works, we are simply not cut out for sensible knavery. Only those who are genuinely honest will be able to resist the temptation to cheat in situations when it would be unwise to do so. Frank explains the psychological mechanism at work here as follows:

> If Smith is emotionally predisposed to regard cheating as an unpleasurable act in and of itself – that is, if he has a conscience – he will be better able to resist the temptation to cheat. If the psychological reward mechanism is constrained to emphasize rewards in the present moment, the simplest counter to a specious reward from cheating is to have a current feeling that tugs in precisely the opposite direction. Guilt is just such a feeling.[24]

The best way to stop oneself from cheating when it would be unwise to do so is to make oneself into the sort of person who values honesty for its own sake. As Frank puts it earlier in his book, "[i]n order to *appear* honest, it may be necessary, or at least very helpful, to *be* honest."[25] The best way to secure happiness is to have a reputation for virtue, and the best way to get such a reputation is to be a genuinely virtuous person. Being a genuinely moral person remains the best bet for securing happiness; this is why we should be moral. So goes the Hume/Frank response.

Here, then, are two objections to the second premise of the moral challenge, two nontheistic answers to the question why be moral? I have described these two responses because I think that each is worthy of serious consideration. Moreover, the existence of such responses shows that those who would argue, as Craig does, that *only* theism offers an adequate response to the challenge have a lot more philosophical work to do. In the end, however, I will not hang my hat on either of these responses. I wish instead to endorse a quite different kind of response to the moral challenge.

3.3   SECOND ANSWER: BECAUSE YOU OUGHT TO

We have considered three ways of objecting to the second premise of the moral challenge: The theistic response; the Aristotelian response; and the Hume/Frank response. But what of the first premise of the challenge? That premise is based on the notion that the only reason there could be for performing a given action is that the action is in one's interest. But it seems to me that such a claim is straightforwardly false. There are many possible different kinds of reason for performing a given action; that it is in one's interest is but one. Another reason for performing an action is simply *that it is morally obligatory for one to do so*.

According to Immanuel Kant (1996), "[T]he greatest perfection of a human being is to do his duty *from duty* (for the law to be not only the rule but also the incentive of his actions)."[26] On Kant's view a virtuous person is one who not only fulfills his moral obligations, but also does so precisely *because* they are his obligations. In his most widely read work on ethics, *Groundwork of the Metaphysic of Morals*, Kant (1964) draws a distinction between *hypothetical imperatives* on the one hand and the *categorical imperative* on the other.[27] Hypothetical imperatives specify the means to a certain end, and apply only to beings who desire the end in question. "If you want to get an A on the next test, start studying now" is a hypothetical imperative, one that is irrelevant to someone who lacks the desire to get an A on the next test. The categorical imperative, by contrast, applies to all rational beings regardless of what their desires are. This is the moral law, a law you must obey regardless of what desires you happen to have.

Corresponding to this distinction among kinds of imperatives is a distinction among kinds of reasons for action. That a given course of action would satisfy one of your desires is one sort of reason for performing an action; that a given course of action is morally obligatory is another sort of reason for performing it. Moreover, on Kant's view, the second kind of reason is the most powerful kind of reason there is. That a given action is morally obligatory trumps all other considerations. Once a person with Kantian virtue discovers an alternative that is morally obligatory, deliberation about how to act is at an end: What to do is clear, all things considered. For Kant, taking duty to be an overriding consideration is a distinctive feature of a morally good person, whereas taking one's self-interest to be the most important consideration is a distinctive feature of a morally bad person:

> [T]he distinction between a good man and one who is evil...must depend upon...*which of the two incentives he makes the condition of the other*. Consequently man...is evil only in that he reverses the moral order of the incentives when he adopts them as his maxim....He makes the incentive of self–love and its inclinations the condition of obedience to the moral law....[28]

An evil person is someone who does his duty just so long as it corresponds to what is in his own best interest. But when self-interest and obligation conflict, the evil person follows self-interest.[29] This is what Kant means when he says that the evil person "makes the incentive of self-love and its inclinations the condition of obedience to the moral law." A good person, on the other hand, does what is in his own best interest – but only as long as it corresponds to what is morally required of him. When self-interest and obligation conflict, the good person does his duty.

All of this suggests a different kind of response to our initial challenge. The response is simply that the fact that a given course of action is morally obligatory is itself a reason – indeed the most powerful kind of reason – for performing the action in question *regardless of whether the action is in one's interest*. More generally, the fact that a given course of action is a way of being moral *is* a reason for performing that action. To the question "why be moral?" a perfectly acceptable answer is "because it is moral." This might seem odd until one notices that to the question "why do what is in one's interest?" a perfectly acceptable answer is "because it is in one's interest." No further explanation is required in either case.

Kant thought that those who seek to justify acting morally on the grounds that morality and self-interest coincide actually do a tremendous disservice to morality:

> Morality must not lower herself. Her own nature must be her recommendation. All else, *even divine reward*, is as nothing beside her. . . . Moral grounds of impulse ought to be presented by themselves and for themselves. . . . Coquetry debauches instead of commending itself, and when ethics plays the flirt she courts the same fate. Beauty, simple and modest, is infinitely more appealing than all the arts and allurements of coquetry. It is the same with moral goodness. It is more potent and appealing in its simple purity than when it is bedecked with allurements, whether of reward or punishment.[30]

Kant sees the attempt to show that we have a reason to fulfill our moral obligations because doing so is in our own interest as a selling-out of morality. We might relate this Kantian point to the moral challenge as follows: Those who seek to respond to the challenge by attacking the second premise are tacitly granting the truth of the first premise. But to accept the first premise is not only to accept what is false; on Kant's view, acceptance of such a premise is more than a cognitive error; it is an *ethical defect*. To think that the only consideration that is relevant in deciding what to do is what will maximize one's interest is to exhibit vicious selfishness. The virtuous person recognizes a class of reasons distinct from those of self-interest: The reasons of morality. That person recognizes, moreover, that reasons of the second kind trump those of the first kind.

In maintaining that we have a reason to care about where our obligations lie only if God exists, Craig assumes that ultimately the only kind of reason there can be to perform a given action is that it is in one's interest to do so. The idea seems to be that unless you will be punished for doing what you ought not to do and rewarded for doing what you ought to do, there is no reason to give a damn about the difference between the two. But this is false and, indeed, indicates a childish view of morality. Grown-ups recognize that the fact that a given action is morally obligatory is itself an overriding reason for performing that action. A morally obligatory action is an action that one *has* to do whether one *wants* to do it or not. Rewards and punishments may provide *additional* reasons for doing what we morally ought to do, but they do not constitute the *only* reasons for doing so. Craig's argument therefore fails.

3.4   THE DIVINE GUARANTEE OF PERFECT JUSTICE AND KANT'S MORAL ARGUMENT

A crucial element of Craig's argument is that the existence of God guarantees a perfectly just universe. I want to explore some of the implications of this notion, beginning with an examination of Kant's use of this concept in an important argument found toward the end of his *Critique of Practical Reason*.

The argument I have in mind appears in the section of the *Critique* titled "The Existence of God as a Postulate of Pure Practical Reason." A key concept in the argument is the highest good, which Kant takes to consist of two main components: (1) Morality, where this consists of all rational beings being morally perfect; and (2) happiness proportional to that morality.[31] It is the second component of the highest good that does the work in the argument at hand, and this component is related to the divine guarantee of perfect justice.

Kant's argument begins from the premise that each of us is morally obligated "to strive to promote the highest good."[32] This amounts to the claim that each of us is obligated to try to bring it about that everyone is morally perfect, and that everyone receives the amount of happiness we deserve. From this premise Kant reasons as follows:

[H]ence there is in us not merely the warrant but also the necessity, as a need connected with duty, to presuppose the possibility of this highest good, which, since it is possible only under the condition of the existence of God, connects the presupposition of the existence of God inseparably with duty; that is, it is morally necessary to assume the existence of God.[33]

Each of us is obligated to pursue the highest good. Yet we cannot sensibly pursue the highest good unless we believe that the highest good is attainable. We cannot sensibly believe that the highest good is attainable unless we believe that there is a being who will make it possible that the highest good comes into existence – and a little reflection reveals that the only being who could accomplish this is God. Hence, we cannot sensibly pursue the highest good unless we believe that God exists. But since we are obligated to pursue the highest good, we must believe that God exists; as Kant puts it, such a belief is "morally necessary." Kant is careful to make it clear that the conclusion of the argument is not that we are morally obligated to believe that God exists, since "there can be no duty to assume the existence of anything."[34] Rather, Kant's desired conclusion seems to be something along these lines: The claim that God exists, while not something we are directly obligated to believe, is a claim we must accept in order sensibly to live up to our obligation to pursue the highest good.

Kant's argument, then, is that atheism interferes with one's ability to fulfill all of one's moral obligations. An atheist cannot rationally pursue the highest good – and yet all human beings are morally obligated to pursue the highest good. So the atheist must either act irrationally (pursuing the highest good while believing it to be unattainable) or do something wrong by neglecting to pursue the highest good. Perhaps Kant believes that the former option is actually psychologically impossible, in which case one can fulfill all of one's moral obligations only if one is a theist.

Kant's argument depends on the claim that the highest good is not attainable on earth. If it were, then we could fulfill our obligation to pursue the highest good without believing in an afterlife in which justice is meted out by a divine judge. At this point I would like to examine some strands of Christian thought that lie behind the idea that Kant's highest good is not attainable in this life.[35] This discussion will serve to highlight some important elements of the Christian view of the universe and will help us to see how the naturalist should respond to Kant's argument.

A central component of the Christian view of the universe is that human beings are morally corrupt as a consequence of the Fall of Man. In the Old Testament, God observes that "the inclination of the human heart is evil from youth."[36] According to C. S. Lewis (2001), one consequence of the Fall is that "man is now a horror to God and to himself."[37] On Kant's view human beings are incapable of attaining moral perfection in this life because of this corruption: "Complete conformity of the will with the moral law is . . . *holiness*, a perfection of which no rational being of the sensible world is capable at any moment of his existence."[38] Holiness includes complete freedom from inclinations pulling us away from the path of duty, but such contrary inclinations cannot be entirely eliminated in this life: "Be a man ever so virtuous, there are in him promptings of evil, and he must constantly contend with these."[39] Consequently, the first component of Kant's highest good – the moral perfection of all rational beings – is unattainable on earth.

A second obstacle to attaining Kant's highest good on earth underlies Jesus' command that we "[D]o not judge, so that you may not be judged."[40] Lewis suggests that we are told not to judge the moral character of others because we are not qualified to do so. A proper evaluation of an individual's moral character would require complete knowledge of that person's inner psychology, heredity, and upbringing – what Lewis calls the raw material. But "[W]e see only the results which a man's choices make out of his raw material. . . . God does not judge him on the raw material at all, but on what he has done with it."[41] Kant makes much the same point, suggesting that "[O]nly God can see that our dispositions are moral and pure."[42]

Kant takes this idea even further: We are not qualified to judge even our own character. Kant maintains that (1) having the right sort of motivation is a component of moral virtue; and (2) we cannot know the nature of our own motives:

> The depths of the human heart are unfathomable. Who knows himself well enough to say, when he feels the incentive to fulfill his duty, whether it proceeds entirely from the representation of the law or whether there are not many other sensible impulses contributing to it that look to one's advantage ... and that, in other circumstances, could just as well serve vice?[43]

Earlier in *The Metaphysics of Morals* Kant rhetorically asks: "[H]ow many people who have lived long and guiltless lives may not be merely *fortunate* in escaping so many temptations?"[44]

This aspect of Kant's view is powerfully illustrated in Joseph Conrad's (1976) novel *The Heart of Darkness*. That novel revolves around the character of Kurtz, a European who enters the Belgian Congo in search of ivory. Kurtz is remarkable in that before he entered the jungle he was widely regarded as a moral man with powerful ideas. His purpose in going into the Congo was not merely to make money, but also to bring civilization to the savages, to bring light into the heart of darkness.

Conrad tells the story from the point of view of the character Marlow, who during his own journey into the Congo becomes increasingly obsessed with Kurtz and sets out to find him. At one point another character offers Marlow the following description of Kurtz:

> "He is a prodigy," he said at last. "He is an emissary of pity, and science, and progress, and devil knows what else. We want," he began to declaim suddenly, "for the guidance of the cause entrusted to us by Europe, so to speak, higher intelligence, wide sympathies, a singleness of purpose."[45]

Later, Marlow finds some of Kurtz's own writing:

> [I]t was a beautiful piece of writing. ... He began with the argument that we whites, from the point of development we had arrived at, "must necessarily appear to them [savages] in the nature of supernatural beings – we approach them with the might as of a deity," and so on, and so on. "By the simple exercise of our will we can exert a power for good practically unbounded," &c., &c. From that point he soared and took me with him. The peroration was magnificent,

83

though difficult to remember, you know. It gave me the notion of an exotic Immensity ruled by an august Benevolence. It made me tingle with enthusiasm.[46]

Kurtz is portrayed as a remarkable man with moral vision and high aspirations, confident both of the quality of his own character and his ability to transform the character of others for the better. Those familiar with the novel know, of course, that Kurtz utterly fails to live up to his own ideals. Instead, by the time Marlow finds Kurtz, he has apparently gone mad, transformed into a power-crazed, blood-thirsty warlord. The natives do indeed seem to view him as a deity of sorts, but there is nothing even remotely resembling "an august Benevolence" in the way he rules them. Kurtz lives in a house in the midst of the jungle surrounded by severed heads on stakes – heads that face inward, toward Kurtz. Marlow reflects on the heads and on Kurtz in these powerful lines:

> [T]here was nothing exactly profitable in these heads being there. They only showed that Mr. Kurtz lacked restraint in the gratification of his various lusts, that there was something wanting in him – some small matter which, when the pressing need arose, could not be found under his magnificent eloquence. Whether he knew of this deficiency himself I can't say. I think the knowledge came to him at last – only at the very last. But the wilderness had found him out early, and had taken on him a terrible vengeance for the fantastic invasion. I think it had whispered to him things about himself which he did not know, things of which he had no conception till he took counsel with this great solitude – and the whisper had proved irresistibly fascinating. It echoed loudly within him because he was hollow at the core. . . . [47]

Kurtz, who in European society seemed moral to everyone including himself, makes an awful discovery about his own character when he finds himself out of society, alone in the jungle, and worshipped as a god. Had he not left European society, he might well have lived a long and guiltless life – but he would have been, in Kant's words, "merely *fortunate* in escaping so many temptations."[48] In the jungle he discovered a lack of restraint within himself, together with dark inclinations he never knew he had. According to Marlow, "His soul was mad. . . . It had looked within itself, and, by heavens! I tell you, it had gone mad."[49] In short, Kurtz discovers within himself a heart of darkness. This is the significance of Kurtz's famous last words – "The horror! The horror!" – which Marlow describes as "a judgment upon the adventures of [Kurtz's] soul upon the earth."[50]

The case of Kurtz illustrates Kant's claim about the difficulty of judging our own character. When Kurtz went into the jungle, he made a *discovery* about himself. He discovered a defect in his character that was present all along, but which would never have been revealed had he not left civilized society. This meshes nicely with Lewis's proposed explanation for Jesus' command to us not to judge others; we simply are not qualified to do so.

If we are not qualified to judge the character of others, and perhaps even our own, then we will be unable to distribute happiness in accordance with desert. What people deserve depends in part on the nature of their moral character. If we cannot accurately judge the character of others, we will be unable to give people what they deserve. Hence, Kant's highest good is unattainable by humans. Only God can make the judgments required to attain the higher good.

A third sort of obstacle to attaining Kant's highest good on earth arises from the problem of evil. In attempting to respond to the problem of evil, at least some Christian writers have put forth views that entail that undeserved suffering on the part of humans is an inevitable feature of the human condition. One prominent example of this appears in Lewis's outstanding book *The Problem of Pain*, which he obviously wrote as a response to the discussion of pain toward the end of Hume's *Dialogues Concerning Natural Religion*. Lewis attempts to explain the presence of pain in the world by suggesting that at least some of the pain is used by God as a means to achieve certain goals. He describes eloquently one of the uses to which God puts pain:

> God, who has made us, knows what we are and that our happiness lies in Him. Yet we will not seek it in Him as long as He leaves us any other resort where it can even plausibly be looked for. While what we call 'our own life' remains agreeable we will not surrender it to Him. What then can God do in our interests but make 'our own life' less agreeable to us, and take away the plausible source of false happiness?[51]

Suppose you have a child who loves to play video games. Your child loves video games so much that he thinks of nothing else; he is perfectly happy to play video games until, as they say, the cows come home. Suppose also that you *know* that your child would be happier – would lead a fuller life – if he were to put aside his video games and devote his energies elsewhere. One way to get him to do this would be to ruin video game playing for him. If you could somehow make the video games boring or unpleasant for him, this would motivate him to look elsewhere for fulfillment.

Lewis's idea is that humans are somewhat like video-game-playing children. We tend to look for happiness and fulfillment in earthly things instead of in God. God knows that our true happiness lies in Him but sees that we will never turn to Him if we remain contented with earthly things. God uses pain to spoil the earthly things for us. This frees us of the illusion that the earthly things hold real happiness for us and inclines us to look elsewhere. One use to which God puts pain, then, is to teach us the lesson that Pascal (1995) puts this way: "Do not look for satisfaction on earth, do not hope for anything from humanity. Your good is only in God, and ultimate happiness lies in knowing God, in becoming united with him for ever in eternity."[52] Lewis notes that this view implies that at least some of the pain God inflicts on human beings is *undeserved* pain. In fact this is one of the strengths of Lewis's proposal as a solution to the problem of evil: It offers an explanation for one of the most troubling kinds of evil – undeserved suffering. Lewis writes:

> We are perplexed to see misfortune falling upon decent, inoffensive, worthy people – on capable, hard-working mothers of families or diligent, thrifty little tradespeople, on those who have worked so hard, and so honestly, for their modest stock of happiness and now seem to be entering on the enjoyment of it with the fullest right. How can I say with sufficient tenderness what here needs to be said? . . . The life to themselves and their families stands between them and the recognition of their need; He makes that life less sweet to them.[53]

As long as humans are inclined to be satisfied with earthly happiness – and, as a consequence of the Fall, they always will be – God will inflict undeserved suffering on them in order to turn them away from false happiness and back toward Himself, the source of true human happiness. Undeserved suffering, consequently, can never be entirely eliminated from our world – God would not permit that to happen:

> A Christian cannot, therefore, believe any of those who promise that if only some reform in our economic, political, or hygienic system were made, a heaven on earth would follow. . . . The settled happiness and security which we all desire, God withholds from us by the very nature of the world. . . . The security we crave would teach us to rest our hearts in this world and oppose an obstacle to our return to God. . . . Our Father refreshes us on the journey with some pleasant inns, but will not encourage us to mistake them for home.[54]

On Lewis's view, Kant's highest good is unattainable on earth because God will not permit it on earth.[55]

What, then, should the naturalist say about Kant's original argument? Is there any way to resist Kant's conclusion that unless one is a theist one cannot fulfill all of one's moral obligations? One way of responding to Kant's argument would be to reject the premise that Kant's highest good is unattainable on earth. But this strategy does not seem particularly promising. Even on the naturalistic view of things there seem to be a number of factors that make the prospects of attaining Kant's highest good pretty dim.

First, even if we would not go as far as Kant in doubting our capacity to estimate the quality of our own moral character, there is surely something to Kant and Lewis's suggestion that we are incapable of making sufficiently precise and accurate judgments about the character of others to determine *exactly* what each person deserves.[56] It seems true that perfect justice on earth is hampered by our inability to arrive at perfect estimations about how others ought to be treated.

Second, there is the problem of moral luck. In a naturalistic universe, many things are outside of our control. Of course this is also true on the theistic view of the universe. But on the naturalistic view, many things are outside of the control of *anyone*. On this view, no one is ultimately in charge of the universe. Despite tremendous advances in medicine and technology, and despite the incredible wealth and power of the wealthiest and most powerful human beings currently alive, bad things sometimes happen to good people and there is nothing anyone can do about it. It seems very unlikely that we could ever get sufficient control over the universe to bring it about that everyone gets what he or she deserves (even if we knew what everyone deserves). This dependency and lack of complete control seems to be an unavoidable condition of human life. As Cottingham (2003) puts it:

> [H]owever far the march of scientific rationality may take us ... it cannot remove the most fundamental aspect of the human condition – our dependency, our finitude, our mortality. Many philosophers show a strange tendency to conceal this bleak reality from themselves by adopting ... a kind of jaunty optimism about the powers of human reason. That science can at best mitigate, but never wholly eradicate, our inherent vulnerability is a fact that they have somehow managed to avoid confronting.[57]

Third, according to naturalism, there is a finite (and, some would say, relatively modest) upper limit on the amount of good a person can receive. At least as things stand now, no human can attain more than something like, say, one hundred thirty years of relatively healthy life filled with all the goods this world has to offer. But it is at least plausible to suppose that some who have lived *deserved* more than this. Might not a Gandhi or a Mother Teresa deserve more than the best earthly human life? Perhaps some even deserve the eternal salvation that Christianity promises. But if naturalism is true, then people in this category simply cannot receive what they deserve. The best the universe can offer them is just not good enough.

A better response to Kant's argument, I think, is to question whether we have the obligation to bring about Kant's highest good. Note that Kant himself actually says only that we are obligated to *"strive to promote* the highest good."[58] According to naturalism, Kant's highest good is unattainable. Therefore, by Kant's famous "ought implies can" principle, we are not obligated to attain the highest good. But we may nevertheless have the obligation to get as close to it as we can. What our obligations are depends in part on what is possible, and what is possible depends in part on whether God exists. If God does exist, then Kant's highest good is attainable, and we may have the obligation to attain it. But if God does not exist, then we cannot have such an obligation – but we can have the obligation to come as close to attaining it as we can. In fact, if God does exist, then at least the second component of Kant's highest good (perfect justice) is not only possible but *certain*. This follows from the feature of theism that played a role in Craig's argument discussed earlier in this chapter – the divine guarantee of perfect justice. This guarantee surely takes at least some of the urgency out of human action: If we know that God will make the universe perfectly just in the end, we lose one reason for trying to promote justice, namely that if we do not, no one will – though we still have a self-interested reason to promote justice, since presumably God rewards the just.[59] Without God in the picture, the universe is only as just as we make it, and consequently there is a much greater urgency to pursue justice here on earth. In fact, the notion that there is a divine guarantee of perfect justice can lead not only to complacency, but to outright atrocity. Such a guarantee also renders one of the most admirable kinds of human action impossible, as we shall see in Section 3.5.

3.5 DIVINE JUSTICE, SELF-SACRIFICE, AND MORAL ABSURDITY

Craig relates the following report by Richard Wurmbrand (1967):

> The cruelty of atheism is hard to believe when man has no faith in the reward of good or the punishment of evil. There is no reason to be human. There is no restraint from the depths of evil which is in man. The Communist torturers often said, 'There is no God, no hereafter, no punishment for evil. We can do what we wish.' I have heard one torturer even say, 'I thank God, in whom I don't believe, that I have lived to this hour when I can express all the evil in my heart.' He expressed it in unbelievable brutality and torture inflicted on prisoners.[60]

At least as compelling as this account is the tale of the massacre of every single occupant of the French city of Beziers in 1209 C.E. The city was taken by Catholic crusaders during the Albigensian Crusade, launched by Pope Innocent III in 1208. This crusade was directed against the Cathars in southern France. The Cathars were heretics who held that all matter was evil and that there were two omnipotent Gods, a good God who had created the invisible world, and an evil God who had created the visible world.[61]

The city of Beziers fell quickly and the crusaders burned it to the ground. They slaughtered its occupants – men, women, and children, catholic and heretic alike. The historian Jonathan Sumption (1978) writes:

> A German monk repeated a story that Arnald-Amaury, when asked in the middle of the slaughter how the catholics could be distinguished from the heretics, replied 'Kill them all; God will recognize his own'; and this motto has passed into history as the epitome of the spirit which had brought the crusaders to the south. Whether Arnald-Amaury was consulted, or ever uttered any such sentiment, remains unclear. But it is not important. The legate reported the massacre without comment to Innocent III, remarking only that 'neither age, nor sex, nor status had been spared.'[62]

Craig points to a case where atheism inspired horrendous behavior; here theism – specifically, the divine guarantee of justice – appears to have done the same.[63] Rather than take a chance on letting some heretics escape, the conquerors opted to hand everyone over to God for judgment, believing (correctly, on the Christian view of things) that God would punish or reward each as was appropriate.[64] Steven Pinker (2002) mentions a more recent example:

> When Susan Smith sent her two young sons to the bottom of a lake, she eased her conscience with the rationalization that "my children deserve to have the best, and now they will." Allusions to a happy afterlife are typical in the final letters of parents who take their children's lives before taking their own....[65]

Like the massacre at Beziers, the notion of a divine guarantee of perfect justice seems to underlie the tragedies Pinker describes. If justice cannot be had on earth, then one recourse for the believer is to put matters directly into God's hands.

The atheist has no such recourse. On the naturalist view of things, the universe is only as just as we make it: There is no divine being to guarantee a just universe, no omniscient judge to whom we can give the difficult cases. The sense that there is no such divine guarantee can inspire a sense of urgency in the quest to obtain justice in this world. It can, moreover, make us more cautious about the taking of human life. The notion that there is a divine guarantee of justice, on the other hand, can make us more careless with human life. It can make us more willing to impose capital punishment, to send our soldiers off to war, and, in the cases of Susan Smith and the crusaders at Beziers, to slaughter the innocent. Perhaps atheism can make some more willing to engage in horrendous actions; the point here is that theism can do the same.

In a universe in which there is a divine guarantee of perfect justice, it is impossible for one person to impose upon another an ultimate fate that the second person does not deserve. In such a universe, no matter what X does to Y now, God will see to it that, in the end, Y gets exactly what Y deserves. Even by killing another person, one does not impose an undeserved ultimate fate upon the victim. In a universe in which there is a divine guarantee of perfect justice, the killer causes the victim to pass into the hands of a perfect Judge, who delivers precisely the fate the victim deserves.

Such a view of the universe can, of course, be a source of tremendous comfort. It can also, as in the case of the massacre at Beziers, inspire tremendous atrocities. The view has another important implication. The implication is that it is impossible for one person to *accept* an ultimate fate that is not deserved, and in so doing prevent another person from enduring an ultimate fate that is not deserved. In particular, the view implies that it is impossible for one person to accept an ultimate fate worse than is deserved, and in so doing prevent *another* person from enduring an ultimate fate worse than is deserved.

We rightly admire those who give their lives so that others may live. Imagine, for example, a mother who sacrifices her own life so that her child can live. If there is a divine guarantee of perfect justice, then the child who lives has not been saved from an undeserved fate, nor has the mother who dies accepted a fate worse than she deserves. But if there is no God – and hence no divine guarantee of perfect justice – the situation is different. In a naturalistic universe, death marks the permanent end of conscious experience, and deprives the individual of any future goods that would have been obtained in life.[66] Without God, the woman who sacrifices her life to save her child may well have accepted a fate worse than the one she deserves, and in so doing she may have spared her child a fate worse than the one it deserves. It follows, therefore, that only in a Godless universe is this kind of self-sacrificing action possible. Only in a Godless universe can one forego the ultimate fate one deserves in order to help others.

It does not follow from this that in a universe in which God exists there is nothing to admire in the actions of those who give their own lives so that others may live. This is true even of those who are certain that they are headed for eternal salvation. There is something to admire in the actions of the claustrophobe who overcomes irrational fears to get into a crowded elevator. Fear in the face of death is a natural human reaction, and there is something to admire in the actions of someone who overcomes this fear – even if it is certain that the fear is unfounded. But there is even more to admire in the actions of someone who knows that death is the end and accepts it anyway for the sake of the greater good. Only without God is this highest form of self-sacrifice, one of the most admirable kinds of human action, an available option. Only without God can a human being – knowing that death is the end, that there is no hope of eternal salvation or divine justice, no chance that he will get the further goods he deserves – nevertheless accept death for himself so that others may live.

In making this argument I am trying, to some extent, to turn the tables on Craig. As we have seen, Craig holds that without God, there is no right and wrong; hence without God, there can be no moral action at all. I have already suggested that Craig is wrong on this point, and my suggestion here is that only if God does *not* exist is one of the most admirable types of moral action possible. It turns out that the absence of God from the universe makes possible one of the most worthy kinds of action a human being can take.

This fact bears on a certain kind of argument for God's existence. This argument, like Kant's argument from the *Critique of Practical Reason*, involves the concept of a divine guarantee of perfect justice.

The argument begins with the claim that here on earth, there is a tremendous amount of injustice. Many who are virtuous suffer and many who are vicious prosper. Those who fulfill their moral obligations are often worse off as a consequence, whereas those who ignore their obligations benefit through their immorality. In a naturalistic universe, there is no afterlife in which all of this injustice can be remedied. Without God and an afterlife, therefore, the universe is fundamentally unjust; in the final tally some who are vicious come out ahead of some who are virtuous. But this simply cannot be. In the words of George Mavrodes (1993), a prominent defender of one version of this argument, a universe that is fundamentally unjust in this fashion is "absurd...a crazy world."[67] Since our universe is not absurd in this way, it must contain God and an afterlife; our universe must contain a divine guarantee of perfect justice. We can infer, therefore, that God does in fact exist. His existence and divine justice prevent the universe from being fundamentally unjust.

This type of argument is ridiculed by Bertrand Russell (1957) in his infamous essay "Why I Am Not a Christian." Russell writes:

> Supposing you got a crate of oranges that you opened, and you found all the top layer of oranges bad, you would not argue, "The underneath ones must be good, so as to redress the balance." You would say, "Probably the whole lot is a bad consignment"; and that is really what a scientific person would say about the universe. He would say, "Here we find in this world a great deal of injustice, and so far as that goes that is a reason for supposing that justice does not rule in the world; and therefore so far as it goes it affords a moral argument against deity and not in favor of one."[68]

Russell rightly questions the premise of the argument that says that the universe must be fundamentally just after all. Perhaps if we had some independent assurance that God exists we could be assured that the universe is fundamentally just – but of course if we had that sort of assurance the argument would be irrelevant. And without such assurance, what reason is there for accepting the premise in question? The argument is either superfluous or unconvincing.

In light of the previous discussion we can make a further criticism of the argument. The further criticism is that the presence of God in the universe renders the type of admirable sacrifice discussed earlier impossible. Might a universe in which this type of action is impossible also be characterized as absurd? If this is right, then the situation is follows: If God does not exist, then the universe is absurd in virtue of being fundamentally unjust. On the other hand, if God does exist, then the universe is absurd in virtue of the fact that admirable sacrifice is impossible. It turns out that the universe must be absurd in some respect, and hence the idea that the universe cannot be absurd loses all plausibility.

3.6 ABSOLUTE EVIL AND MORAL FAITH

Still another variation on Kant's argument appears in Gordon Graham's (2001) challenging book *Evil and Christian Ethics*. Graham's argument, in outline, is that we can rationally accept the existence of what he calls "absolute evil" only if we presuppose that God exists. Since absolute evil is real, we ought to accept its existence; hence, if we do not presuppose that God exists, we are being irrational.

Graham's claim that absolute evil exists has two components. One component is the claim that the fact that a given course of action is morally obligatory for a given person entails that the person has an overriding reason to perform the action in question – a reason that trumps all other considerations.[69] The action *must* be performed, all things considered. The second component is the claim that there is at least one type of action such that it is always morally wrong for anyone to perform an action of that type (or, alternatively, that everyone always has a moral obligation to refrain from performing actions of that type). As Graham puts it, there are "*some* ways of treating human beings that are indeed absolutely forbidden."[70] Graham offers slavery as an example.[71]

The argument, then, or at any rate one strand of it, seems to run as follows: The existence of absolute evil entails the real possibility that a person might land in a situation in which doing what is morally obligatory leads, as far as anyone can see, to both personal ruin and widespread disaster. But no one can rationally accept the possibility of a situation in which following an obligatory course of action would lead both to personal ruin and widespread disaster. Therefore, a person can rationally accept the existence of absolute evil only if she has moral faith, which Graham characterizes as follows: "[I]t is faith in the truth of two propositions: (i) acting morally is in my interests even when I do not and cannot know this; (ii) morality will not ultimately conflict with personal or social well-being, appearances to the contrary notwithstanding."[72]

Let us consider the first component of moral faith – faith that morality and one's self-interest ultimately coincide. Graham's claim is that we cannot rationally accept the existence of absolute evil unless we have this sort of faith. And we can have this sort of faith only if we have faith that God exists. This is supposed to be true for the now-familiar reason that only if God exists is there a divine guarantee of perfect justice, and without such a guarantee it is possible that morality and self-interest will not coincide.

Whether Graham's argument succeeds or not seems to depend on the correct answer to this question: Is it really *irrational* to believe that one might find oneself in a situation in which fulfilling one's moral obligations leads to personal ruin – *period*? Is it really irrational to believe that self-interest and duty might conflict in such a strong fashion? Well, one man's irrationality is another's truism; all I can do is register my view that believing this is not irrational in the slightest. Indeed, it strikes me that it is one of the more obvious features of moral experience. *Of course* morality and self-interest can conflict in this strong way; *of course* it is possible to face a situation in which doing one's duty will lead to personal ruin. So, if it turns out that the only way aliens can be stopped from enslaving every human being on the face of the earth is for you to sell everything you own, give away the money, and live on the streets then tough luck indeed; let the auction begin! Responding to these sorts of situations properly, making the required sacrifices, taking one for the team – this is the essence of moral action. There is certainly nothing irrational in recognizing the possibility of these kinds of cases. Perhaps part of the initial plausibility, if any, of Graham's claim is derived from supposing that all we know about the action that leads to personal ruin is that it is morally obligatory. But this is rarely if ever the case;

typically, when we know *that* an action is morally obligatory we have at least some inkling of *why* it is morally obligatory.[73] Once I realize that it is only through personal ruin that I can save the human race, I can see quite easily why I *must* bring about my own personal ruin.

What about the possibility that fulfilling one's obligations might lead to disaster not just for oneself but on a much wider scale? My response here is that if the disaster in question is sufficiently disastrous, it can indeed be irrational to believe that one is morally obligated to act in such a way as to bring about the disaster. But I think that in cases of this sort, the obligation in question does not in fact exist. This point needs elaboration.

In explaining Graham's notion of "absolute evil," I distinguished two components of it. The reason for this will now become clear; I think that we should accept the first component but reject the second. It turns out that absolute evil in Graham's sense does not exist. Earlier I discussed the Kantian view that moral reasons trump all other kinds of reason, and the fact that a given action is morally obligatory constitutes an overriding reason for performing that action. I think that this is correct, and this component of what Graham calls "absolute evil" is real. What should be rejected is the claim that there are some types of action such that they are always, under any circumstances, wrong to perform. If it turns out that the only way you can stop the aliens from slowly torturing to death every other human on the face of the planet is by enslaving one person, then you should enslave that one. Slavery is wrong in most circumstances and should be undertaken only as a last resort, but there are possible circumstances in which it is permissible. If the consequences of not enslaving someone are bad enough, one could be obligated to engage in slavery. One need not be a consequentialist to recognize that consequences are always relevant to some extent, and that sufficiently good or bad consequences can, in principle, render any type of action morally right or wrong.

Graham's concept of absolute evil incorporates two distinct aspects of Kantian moral philosophy. One is the notion of moral requirements as overriding; the other is the existence of what Kant calls "perfect duties." Kant somewhat notoriously claims, for instance, that we have a perfect duty to refrain from lying – that it is always, under any circumstances, morally wrong to lie.[74] I think that Kant is right about the overriding nature of moral requirements, but wrong about the existence of perfect duties. We should accept Kant's claim about the *importance* of morality, but we should reject at least some of his claims about its *content*.

3.7 WHERE WE ARE NOW

It is useful to pause briefly here and take stock of the argument so far. I have criticized a variety of arguments aimed at attaching various unattractive ethical implications to naturalism. I have suggested that even if God does not exist, some human lives have internal meaning and that we have various moral obligations. I have criticized certain conceptions of the relationship between God and ethics and outlined the basic elements of what I think is a more promising view. I have argued that even if God does not exist, not only do we have certain moral obligations, but furthermore we have good reason to be concerned with what these moral obligations are. The reason we should care about our obligations is just that *they are our obligations*. This component of Kant's moral philosophy is fundamentally correct, although, as I have just argued, the notion that we have "perfect duties" in the Kantian sense should be rejected.

Next I will turn to the question of ethical character. Specifically, I will consider whether there is a place in a naturalistic universe for virtues like humility, charity, and hope, and I argue that there is. I will describe naturalistic versions of these virtues and in the course of this will outline certain key elements of Christian thought. I will point to some important similarities and differences between the naturalistic view of the universe and the Christian view and conclude with a discussion of whether naturalism is a creed by which we can live.

FOUR

ETHICAL CHARACTER IN
A GODLESS UNIVERSE

4.1 A NEW ASSUMPTION

For the purposes of this chapter it will be useful to introduce a
new assumption, one I have not made prior to this point: We *know
that naturalism is true*. It is important to see that this claim is introduced only as an *assumption*. My purpose here is not to argue for
the truth of naturalism, but rather to examine some of the consequences for ethics of naturalism being true – and not just *being* true
but being *known* to be true. The central topic of this chapter is ethical
character.

What sort of character one ought to strive to inculcate in oneself
and others depends in part on what one knows about the nature of
the universe. Being an ethically good person is, in part, a matter of
being properly oriented toward the universe. A trait that would be a
virtue in one kind of universe might well be a vice in another, and
vice versa. In this chapter I try to describe some virtues in a universe
in which naturalism is known to be true.

4.2 THE FALL OF MAN: PRIDE AND DISOBEDIENCE

The Christian universe is a hierarchical one with a distinct peck-
ing order: God at the top, down through the various orders of angels, human beings, and animals. Each being has a particular station
and role to play. God has dominion over all other beings; humans
have dominion over "the fish of the sea . . . the birds of the air . . . the

98

cattle . . . and all the wild animals of the earth."[1] After the Fall, at any rate, husbands are to rule over their wives.[2] The Christian Bible is, in part, an account of the role assigned to human beings by God, together with the perils of deviating from this assigned role. In this scheme, it is extremely important both that human beings recognize their assigned stations and roles in the universe and that they not attempt to rise above them.

The Fall of Man resulted from just such an attempt. In the Biblical account of the Fall, the serpent portrays God as a deceitful tyrant who, in an attempt to keep them down, lies to Adam and Eve about the consequences of eating from the tree of knowledge:

> The woman said to the serpent, "We may eat of the fruit of the trees in the garden; but God said, 'You shall not eat of the fruit of the tree that is in the middle of the garden, nor shall you touch it, or you shall die.'" But the serpent said to the woman, "You will not die; for God knows that when you eat of it your eyes will be opened, and you will be like God, knowing good and evil.[3]

In Milton's more detailed account of the Fall, the serpent is actually the Devil in disguise who, having learned the hard way the futility of direct confrontation with God, has resorted to deception. He assures Eve that "God cannot . . . hurt ye, and be just" and that He has forbidden Adam and Eve from eating from the tree "to keep ye low and ignorant."[4] A bit later, the Devil even suggests that it is envy on the part of God that motivates Him to try to keep the humans down.[5] In both the Genesis and *Paradise Lost* versions of the Fall, it is Eve's desire to transcend her place in the universe – specifically, to be like God with respect to *knowledge of good and evil* – that leads to disaster. In Milton's extended account, the ultimate cause of all evil is the Devil's failed coup d'etat. Satan and a host of other angels revolted against God's rule; battle ensued, and the upstarts were ultimately defeated and cast into hell. This led Satan to utter his famous line: "Better to reign in hell, than serve in heaven."[6] Again, the source of all the trouble is the refusal to accept one's proper place in the hierarchy.

In Lewis's account of the Fall, which he describes as "a 'myth' in the Socratic sense, a not unlikely tale," the Fall is also due to an attempt by humans to rise above their proper station and become like God.[7] But Lewis makes an alternative suggestion about the respect in which the humans strove to become like God:

> [S]ooner or later they fell. Someone or something whispered that they could become as gods – that they could cease directing their lives to their Creator.... As a young man wants a regular allowance from his father which he can count on as his own, within which he makes his own plans... so they desired to be on their own, to take care for their own future, to plan for pleasure and for security.... They wanted some corner in the universe of which they could say to God, 'This is our business, not yours.' But there is no such corner.[8]

In the Genesis and *Paradise Lost* accounts of the Fall, humans strive to become like God by knowing good and evil. In Lewis's account of the Fall, humans strive to become like God by becoming self-sufficient, independent, and self-governing – at least with respect to some "corner in the universe." Common to both accounts is *disobedience of God's commands in an attempt to rise above one's proper place in the universe.*

As punishment for the attempt to move up the hierarchy, human beings are instead moved down. Initially immortal, they are made mortal. In the Biblical account, the final component of the punishment is the death sentence: God decrees that all human beings will eventually turn back into the dust from which they were formed.[9] In Lewis's version, as punishment for the attempt to become self-sufficient, human beings are made even *more* dependent upon God. Whereas before, human beings had enjoyed complete control over their own bodies and minds, as a consequence of the Fall they lose that control to some extent:

> [T]he organs, no longer governed by man's will, fell under the control of ordinary biochemical laws and suffered whatever the inter–workings of those laws might bring about in the way of pain, senility, and death. And desires began to come up into the mind of man, not as his reason chose, but just as the biochemical and environmental facts happened to cause them.[10]

Pascal, writing from a God's-eye point of view, puts it this way:

> Humans wanted to make themselves the centre of their own atten-
> tion and to be independent of my help. They took themselves away
> from my dominion and, wanting to find happiness in making them-
> selves my equal by finding their happiness in themselves, I left them to
> themselves. I turned into rebates all the creatures who were subject to
> them and provoked them with hostility, so that today human beings
> have become like beasts. . . . [11]

Initially given dominion over all the wild beasts, human beings become like wild beasts themselves. Another consequence of the Fall,
discussed in Chapter 3, is the moral corruption of humanity. Alvin
Plantinga describes that corruption this way:

> [W]e human beings, apart from God's special and gracious activity,
> are sunk in sin; we are prone to hate God and our neighbor; our
> hearts, as Jeremiah said, are deceitful above all things and desperately
> corrupt. [12]

According to Augustine (1993) this moral corruption is present from
birth: "Thus the innocence of children is in the helplessness of their
bodies rather than any quality in their minds. I have myself seen a
small baby jealous; it was too young to speak, but it was livid with
anger as it watched another infant at the breast." [13] With the Fall
of Man, then, "a new species, never made by God, had sinned itself
into existence." [14] This new species is "a horror to God." [15] It is morally
corrupt and selfish. In Lewis's words, it has "turned from God and
become its own idol." [16] Human beings have been damaged not only
morally but also cognitively – so much so that they cannot even know
that God exists without His help. [17] Without God's assistance we are,
according to Pascal, "the equivalent of brute beasts." [18] Without God,
we can become neither happy nor good, and are condemned instead
to evil, misery, and ignorance.

Against this background we can understand the importance
within Christian ethics of obedience to God and why pride is counted
among the seven deadly sins. Jerome Neu (1999) writes that pride is
"the sin of not knowing one's place and sticking to it. It is . . . Faust's
ambitious sin. Challenging God – going above your place." [19] Sinful

pride – an overestimation of one's proper place in the hierarchy, or the attempt to rise above that place – is linked with a loss of respect for God, and consequently with a tendency to disobey God's commands. For creatures like us, who naturally tend toward evil and misery, there is no greater danger than a loss of respect for God's rules for us. This is why a recognition and acceptance of our place in the universe is of central importance in Christian ethics. This recognition is necessary for proper respect for God, which is necessary for obedience, which is necessary for virtue, knowledge, happiness, and salvation. As the Apostle Paul says, "obeying the commandments of God is everything."[20] Perhaps this is why Quinn writes:

> I am of the opinion that Christian moral philosophers ought to join Aquinas in holding that virtue consists chiefly in conformity with God's will and obedience to his commands. As I see it, this should be the ruling idea of any account of the virtues that claims that it is part of genuinely Christian ethics.[21]

And perhaps this is why some Christian writers have sought to understand the moral obligations of human beings entirely in terms of obedience to divine commands.[22]

4.3 HUMILITY, CHRISTIAN AND NATURALISTIC

If naturalism is known to be true, then of course the Biblical account of the Fall is a mere myth. There is no God whom we ought to obey; there is no place in a hierarchy to which we have been divinely assigned. In a naturalistic universe, Christian humility and obedience have no place. What, if anything, takes their place? In a naturalistic universe, are there any virtues that correspond to Christian humility and obedience?

We may approach these questions by considering what the pagan philosopher Aristotle has to say about pride and humility. We have already seen one area of contrast between the Aristotelian view and the Christian view. In Chapter 1, I noted that, on Aristotle's view, the intrinsically best sort of activity of which human beings are capable is theoretical contemplation – the very activity in which the gods are continuously engaged. The philosopher alone can transcend the individual's place in the universe and become, however briefly, like a god. Moreover, this is something for which one should strive and for which one deserves praise. On the Christian view, as we have seen, just the opposite is true. Attempting to transcend one's place in the universe is a sin, something to be avoided at all costs.

The issue of the proper attitude to have toward oneself and one's accomplishments reveals another contrast between the Aristotelian and Christian views. One of the most controversial of the Aristotelian virtues is the virtue of "high-mindedness," or "greatness of soul" (*megalopsychia*). According to Aristotle, a high-minded person is one who "thinks he deserves great things and actually deserves them."[23] What one deserves is to be understood in terms of which external goods are due one. The greatest of the external goods is honor; therefore, high-mindedness has primarily to do with honor. A high-minded person is someone who believes correctly that he deserves a tremendous amount of honor.[24] Because a person cannot deserve great honors without being thoroughly virtuous, one cannot have the virtue of high-mindedness unless one has all the other ethical virtues as well. For this reason Aristotle declares that high-mindedness is "the crown ... of the virtues: it magnifies them and it cannot exist without them."[25] One of the more notable features of Aristotle's discussion of this virtue is the remark that "[a] high-minded person is justified in looking down upon others for he has the right opinion of them."[26] It is undoubtedly remarks like this that lead Alasdair MacIntyre (1998) to characterize Aristotle's account of high-mindedness as an "appalling picture."[27]

It is useful to contrast Aristotle's account with a much more recent secular account of modesty. According to Julia Driver (2001) modesty is a virtue, and "the modest person underestimates his self-worth. ... He underrates himself, and therefore only takes a portion of the credit due him."[28] Driver also says that "for a person to be modest, she must be ignorant with regard to her self-worth. She must think herself less deserving, or less worthy, than she actually is."[29] The trait that Driver calls "modesty" is roughly the Aristotelian vice of "small-mindedness" (*mikropsychia*): "One who underestimates himself is small-minded regardless of whether his actual worth is great or moderate, or ... small."[30]

Driver's proposed account of modesty is also strikingly similar to an account of humility that the devil Screwtape encourages his nephew Wormwood to foist upon his "patient" (victim) in Lewis's (1996) *The Screwtape Letters*:

> You must therefore conceal from the patient the true end of Humility. Let him think of it ... as a certain kind of opinion (namely, a low opinion) of his own talents and character. Some talents, I gather, he really has. Fix in his mind the idea that humility consists in trying to believe those talents to be less valuable than he believes them to be.[31]

Evil demon that he is, Screwtape aims at deception, and the account of humility in question is intended to be a false one. What is the point of getting humans to accept such an account of humility? Screwtape explains:

> The great thing is to make him value an opinion for some quality other than truth, thus introducing an element of dishonesty and make– believe into the heart of what otherwise threatens to become a virtue. By this method thousands of humans have been brought to think that humility means pretty women trying to believe they are ugly and clever men trying to believe they are fools. And since what they are trying to believe may, in some cases, be manifest nonsense, they cannot succeed in believing it, and we have the chance of keeping their minds endlessly revolving on themselves in an effort to achieve the impossible.[32]

Two desirable results (from Screwtape's point of view) of promul- gating the false view of humility are described here. One method of soul corruption that Screwtape often encourages Wormwood to make use of is instilling in humans the habit of holding the views they do, not because the views are true, but rather for some other reason.[33] According to Screwtape's false account, humility involves doing precisely this, and hence getting a human who wants to be- come virtuous to accept such a view is a good way of promoting the desired habit in him.

Second, Screwtape notes that attaining this false humility is often extremely difficult or impossible, and a would-be virtuous human who accepts the view will find himself running in endless circles in the attempt to become humble. The devilish "benefits" of this are obvious: A distraction from genuine virtue, and perhaps ultimately disillusionment and despair.

Of course, even if Screwtape is correct about these consequences, it does not follow that the account of humility in question is *false* (though Screwtape – and Lewis – plainly think that it is). To conclude that the account is false we would need a further premise along these lines: If a given account of some virtue is such that those who accept it tend to be worse off than those who do not accept it, then the account is false. And I see no reason to accept such a premise; perhaps learning the truth can make one worse off?

We have, then, Lewis and Aristotle on one side and Driver on the other. Driver maintains that underestimating one's worth and what one deserves is a virtue, whereas Lewis and Aristotle maintain that this is a vice (or at least not a virtue). I think that it is Lewis and Aristotle who are correct here. First, we may note that ignorance is a kind of a defect, and so Driver holds the paradoxical-sounding view that some virtues, the so-called virtues of ignorance, essentially involve defects. On this view, a fully virtuous person necessarily suffers from certain cognitive defects. Surely this constitutes a prima facie reason for rejecting Driver's view. At the very least, a convincing argument would be required to make it reasonable to accept such a counterintuitive account.

Second, and more importantly, Driver's proposed account of modesty is open to refutation by counterexample. Consider the case of "Amazing Bob." Amazing Bob is the smartest, strongest, most athletic, best-looking person in the universe. Amazing Bob, let us suppose, underestimates his own self-worth. He thinks that he is roughly the one-hundredth smartest, strongest, most athletic and attractive person in the universe. But Amazing Bob constantly brags about how strong, athletic, and attractive he is. Indeed, it is hard to get him to talk or even think about anything outside of his own greatness. For example, each time he meets someone new, he says, "Hi there, I'm Amazing Bob! I'm the one-hundredth smartest, strongest, most athletic and attractive person in the universe! I'm one in a million, baby!" According to Driver's account of modesty, Amazing Bob is modest. But this is plainly false. One may have the trait Driver identifies and yet be a complete braggart. Therefore, the trait Driver identifies is not the virtue of modesty.

By way of Screwtape, Lewis presents his take on the truth about humility:

> The Enemy [God] wants to bring the man to a state of mind in which he could design the best cathedral in the world, and know it to be the best, and rejoice in the fact, without being any more (or less) or otherwise glad at having done it than he would be if it had been done by another. The Enemy wants him . . . to be so free from any bias in his own favour that he can rejoice in his own talents as frankly and *gratefully* as in his neighbour's talents – or in a sunrise, an elephant, or a waterfall.[34]

The view suggested here is that being humble is not a matter of underestimating one's own worth and accomplishments, but rather a matter of *giving proper credit* for the worth and accomplishments. A humble person may have an accurate estimate of his or her own worth. What makes a person humble is the belief that ultimately it is God, at least in large part, who deserves the credit for individual worth and accomplishment. This belief manifests itself in gratefulness toward God. This is the importance of the last line of the passage – humble people see their own admirable features much the way they see other admirable things in the world that have nothing to do with them. People who think that they and they alone deserve *all* the credit and praise for their worth and accomplishments are mistaken – and exhibit a vice. There is a certain ridiculousness to this sort of pride; it is as if a painting were to give all the credit for its beauty to itself and none to its painter.

On this view of humility, there is an important connection between humility and obedience. A humble person recognizes the individual's dependence on God, and so, at least to some extent, is aware of having been assigned a place in the universe. Certainly a humble person would not be so foolish as to feel completely self-sufficient. Moreover, humility engenders gratefulness to God for one's accomplishments (as well as for the accomplishments of others). As I noted in Chapter 2, gratefulness to God is often offered as a reason why we should obey God's commands. Humility, then, ought to produce obedience of God's commands. A prideful person, by contrast, may feel no dependence on God and see no reason to be grateful to Him, and hence may see no reason to obey God's commands. All of this makes humility a crucially important virtue in Christian ethics.

Of course, the naturalist must reject this account of humility (or, failing that, must reject the claim that humility is a virtue), inextricably linked as it is with belief in God. Nevertheless, the account is useful because it helps us to see a problem in Aristotle's position that *megalopsychia* is a virtue and it points us in the direction of what I think is a promising naturalistic account of the virtue of humility.

Aristotle declares that "[g]ifts of fortune ... contribute to high–mindedness. Men of noble birth, of power, or of wealth are regarded as worthy of honor, since they occupy a superior position."[35] Here Aristotle claims that people deserve goods in virtue of factors over which they have no control – in virtue of having received certain "gifts of fortune." Suppose that Smith and Jones are alike in every respect except that Smith is fortunate in having been born into a wealthy and prominent family, whereas Jones has been born into a poor and obscure family. According to Aristotle, in virtue of this difference between the two, Smith deserves more honor and goods than does Jones. If Aristotle were correct, then Smith would be correct in feeling superior and more deserving of honor than Jones precisely by virtue of Smith's "noble birth." But this is mere snobbery and foolishness. In Lewis's view, virtuous Smith would not feel more deserving of goods than Jones does because of the difference between them; instead, Smith would be grateful to God for being born noble. The naturalist can – and should – agree with the first part of this claim.

Suppose that you know naturalism to be true. What, then, is the proper attitude for you to have toward yourself and your own accomplishments? One possible answer is that if all that exists consists entirely of the natural universe, then this leaves humans at the top of the heap. Strip away God and the angels, and humans are the kings of the universe, ruled by no one, and authorized to rule over everything there is. But this is silly; the naturalistic universe is not just the Christian universe in which that section of the hierarchy above human beings has simply been sliced away. Rather, in a naturalistic universe, there is no such hierarchy in the first place. There is no divinely ordered station to which we, or any other creature, has been assigned. Human beings were not singled out for special attention by a divine creator; rather, we were, like every other living thing on earth, formed by blind natural processes entirely beyond our control. This, together with our current state of knowledge of how the natural universe functions and a little careful reflection, suggests something like the following view.

Each of us is spit out into the universe into a set of circumstances not of our choosing, endowed with psychological and physical characteristics and potentialities bestowed on us by factors beyond our control. We have no say over whether to exist at all, or under what circumstances, or with what capacities to be endowed. And yet it is beyond doubt that our circumstances, together with our various capacities, determine what it is possible for us to achieve, and, at least to a large extent, what we in fact do achieve. The nature versus nurture debate rages on – but does anyone seriously question whether these two together do not largely shape our destinies? Reflect on your own life. Consider the family you were born into, the country, the political system, the time, the financial situation, the neighbors that happened to surround you, the schools you happened to attend, the friends you happened to make. Is it possible to overestimate the sum total of the impact these things had on the course of your life?[36]

Some may rightly observe that they have achieved much more than others with similar backgrounds. No one else from *my* neighborhood became a doctor, after all, someone might think. And what was it about you that made the difference? Were you more intelligent? More hard-working? Did you have a more positive attitude? And then consider this question: How much say did you have in whether you were smarter, more hard-working, more optimistic than all the rest? Can you seriously maintain that *all* of it – or even much of it – was of your own making?

Research in social psychology suggests that apparently trivial features of the situations in which we find ourselves can dramatically influence our behavior.[37] Whether or not people will help others is very heavily influenced by the extent to which they are in a hurry and by their general mood, which can be significantly impacted by such minor events as finding (or failing to find) a dime in a public telephone.[38] Apparently normal, well-adjusted, non-violent people will commit sadistic acts and inflict (what they believe to be) tremendous suffering on others as a consequence of firm insistence on the part of an authority figure or, in an other infamous experiment, as a result of being randomly assigned the role of guard in a simulated prison.[39] Such experiments support the central thesis that underlies the account of naturalistic humility I will develop, which is that the impact on ourselves and our lives of factors outside of our control is enormous and far beyond what we tend unreflectively to take it to be. Reflection on such experiments leads John Doris to claim:

> Had I lived in Germany, Rwanda, or any number of places during the wrong historical moment, I might have led a life that was morally reprehensible, despite the fact that the life I lead now is perhaps no worse than morally mediocre. There, but for the grace of God, do I.[40]

As Lewis observes, humility has to do with giving credit where credit is due. It is the *dependence* of human beings that makes humility an appropriate attitude. In Lewis's scheme, we are dependent on God. But a similar sort of dependence is present in the naturalistic universe. In both kinds of universe, the fate of human beings (at least in this life) is largely dependent upon factors outside of their control. In the theistic universe, these factors are ultimately all under God's control, and hence much of the credit for any human accomplishment should go to God. In the naturalistic universe, by contrast, these factors are ultimately under the control of *no one* – and hence much of the credit for any human accomplishment should go to ... well, *no one*. It is not as if with God out of the picture, all the credit for human accomplishments somehow accrues to humans by default; these accomplishments remain just as dependent on factors beyond their control as ever.

One problem with Aristotle's account of high-mindedness is the suggestion that it is appropriate for people to think they deserve praise for certain "gifts of fortune" – factors outside of individual control. But this is just an extreme and obvious version of the sort of mistake made by people who think they deserve *all* the credit for their personal accomplishments – overlooking the large contribution made to their achievements by factors beyond individual control, or mistakenly thinking they somehow deserve credit for factors for which they are in no way responsible.

Lewis also observes that humility has to do with how we view our own accomplishments relative to the accomplishments of others. The humble person, as characterized by Lewis, is entirely free of any personal bias. I take it that Lewis's idea is that the humble person recognizes that there is no advantage to be gained by exaggerating one's own accomplishments since, like the accomplishments of everyone else, they are gifts from God. This allows an honest self-view, which forestalls boastful exaggeration. Even if, like Amazing Bob, a person is truly remarkable, boasting makes no sense because it is ultimately God who was responsible. As the Apostle Paul says, "What do you have that you did not receive? And if you received it, why do you boast as if it were not a gift?"[41] Amazing Bob, if he is humble, will be grateful rather than boastful.

In a naturalistic universe, each of us should recognize the tremendous contribution *dumb luck* has made to all human accomplishments, and that in the case of any such accomplishment, the majority of the credit goes to blind chance. With or without God, puffing oneself up over one's fellow human beings because of one's accomplishments is foolishness. Whatever contribution we might have made to our successes, a far greater contribution was made by factors beyond our control. Consider the most unfortunate, pathetic person of whom you have knowledge. In a naturalistic universe, you should not think to yourself, "There but for the grace of God go I," but instead, "There but for dumb luck go I" – or perhaps, "How lucky that *I* should have existed at all!" God or no God, the concept of a completely self-made individual is a ridiculous fantasy.

What is the relevance to this discussion of the interminable debate about the existence and nature of human free will? If naturalism is true, we know that there is no extranatural soul, no nonphysical true self distinct from the physical self. Suppose, nevertheless, that the natural universe contains within it enough indeterminacy to allow for the presence of free will of a suitably strong sort, so-called "libertarian" free will. Suppose that we can, to some extent, shape our own character through our own free actions. In this way, we may be partially responsible for some of our own actions and even for some aspects of our character.

Well, if we do have libertarian freedom, it is just one more gift of fortune that fell into our laps through blind chance. More importantly, however, we must see that even under the assumption that we have libertarian freedom, the notion of an action for which a human being could be *uniquely responsible*, deserving of *all* the praise or blame for its performance, is pure fiction. *Any* action – any success or failure – depends for its occurrence in large part on factors beyond the control of its agent. Every action we perform, every thought we think, takes place within a framework not of our own making. This framework sets the scope of possibility for us. Even with libertarian freedom in the universe, more of the credit for our accomplishments goes to factors outside of our control than to us.

I am not suggesting that no life is better, more admirable, or more worthwhile than another, or that all human beings really are equal in every way, or that no action is more important or impressive than another. The successful artist who has just painted a masterpiece knows full well that painting is more of an accomplishment than spending the day in a gutter. The masterpiece is surely greater, and merits more admiration and praise, than does the activity of a drunk. What I am suggesting is that the artist's reaction to all of this ought to be a theist's sense of gratitude to God or a naturalist's sense of being very lucky.

It also does not follow from my view that we ought not punish anyone for performing wrong actions or breaking the law. In connection with this point it is important to notice two things. First, responsibility for an action is something that admits of degree; a person may be more or less responsible for a given action. Second, that a person is responsible for a given action *to some extent* often makes it sensible and just to punish the person for performing the action in question: I need not have created the gun and bullets myself, designed my own hair-trigger temper, and conjured up the obnoxious victim in order for it to be sensible and just to punish me for murder. My account of humility depends on the claim that much of the credit for our accomplishments goes to factors beyond our control; this in no way implies that our practices of punishing people for some of their actions should be abolished.

It is the dependence of human beings and their actions on factors beyond their control – dependence that is present whether God exists or not – that makes humility in some form an appropriate attitude to have. In a theistic universe, recognition of our dependence should engender gratefulness toward God; in a naturalistic universe, it should engender a sense of being lucky (in those who have accomplished much). In either sort of universe, taking the balance of the credit for one's accomplishments is foolish. There is indeed such a thing as naturalistic humility, and it is a virtue.[42]

4.4 FROM HUMILITY TO CHARITY

Imagine millions of human beings parachuting down to the surface of an alien planet. The terrain and habitability of the planet's surface varies widely, and so the range of circumstances in which these humans finds themselves upon landing is similarly varied. Some people land in quicksand and find themselves struggling for survival; others land in lush forests, surrounded by ample water and delicious fruit. Still others land in harsh and barren deserts, and so on. We are like these humans in the respect that was the focus of the Section 4.3: What our lives are like depends in large measure on circumstances beyond our control. Like them, we can exert some control over the course of our lives, but the range of possibilities for us is largely out of our hands.

Let us consider two ways of expanding this scenario. First, suppose that these parachuting humans know that an omnipotent, omniscient, and morally perfect being is in charge of the entire affair. This being has designed and created the planet and has decided in advance where each human will land. The being has a master plan, and each human is to play a small but crucial part in that plan. Given these further assumptions, the question I would like to focus on is, what obligations, if any, do the better-off among these humans have to the worse-off? Does a human who lands in a lush forest have any obligation to assist a nearby human who lands in a barren desert?

The answer is not clear; after all, the better-off humans might reflect that the worse-off humans have been placed where they are – have been made worse off – by a perfect being. Such a being would not put these less-fortunate humans in difficult circumstances unless there was a good reason to do so – and who are we to interfere with the perfect being's master plan? Without any further information, the fortunate ones might reasonably conclude that what they ought to do is be grateful for their own fates and leave the others to theirs. "Everyone for himself, God for us all" seems to be a reasonable principle to adopt in the imagined situation.

But let us add one more feature to this scenario. Suppose that the perfect being has issued the following command to the humans: "You shall love your neighbor as yourself."[43] This, it would seem, changes the situation entirely. Given this commandment, the gratefulness that the more fortunate among the humans rightly feel toward the perfect being ought to translate into obedience. Given the commandment to love their neighbors, the better-off among the humans have an obligation to help the worse-off to at least some degree.

The expanded version of the scenario is like the situation that Christians take themselves to be in. There are two things of particular interest here. First, it seems that without the command from God to assist one's neighbors, humans would (arguably) not be under any moral obligation to do so. This suggests another kind of argument for Karamazov's Thesis – that if God does not exist, then all human actions are morally permissible and human beings have no moral obligations at all.[44] Supposing that God does in fact exist, the argument starts with the claim for which I just argued, namely (1) if God had not commanded humans to help their neighbors, we would have no obligation to do so. It might be further observed that (2) if God did not exist, then God would not have commanded humans to

113

help their neighbors. It might be thought that from (1) and (2) we can infer (3) if God did not exist, then we would have no obligation to help our neighbors. Finally, if we add the premise that all of our obligations are relevantly like this one, we get the conclusion that if God did not exist, we would have no obligations – Karamazov's Thesis.

This argument goes wrong in the inference from (1) and (2) to (3). This is an inference of the following form: (1) If Q were true, then R would be true; (2) If P were true, then Q would be true; therefore, (3) If P were true, then R would be true. But the conclusion does not follow from the premises, as can be seen by way of the following counterexample. It happens that I have just one sibling – a brother. Consider the following line of reasoning: (1) If my brother had not been born, then I would be an only child; (2) If my parents had never met, my brother would not have been born; therefore, (3) If my parents had never met, I would be an only child. Claims (1) and (2) are both true, yet (3) clearly is not. The problem is that if my parents had never met, while it is true that my brother would not have been born, certain other things would be true that would make it false that I am an only child – obviously I would not have existed at all.[45] As I will suggest soon, something similar is true in the case of the claim that if God did not exist, then He would not have commanded us to help our neighbors. This is true – but if God does not exist, then certain other things are true that make it the case that we do have an obligation to help our neighbors, despite not having been commanded to do so by God.

The second thing of interest in the forest or desert scenario is that it allows us to see that humility is the basis of at least one component of charity.[46] As I have suggested, humility involves a recognition of one's proper place in the universe and it engenders gratefulness toward God for the good things that one has. Humility, then, leads to the recognition that one ought to obey God's commands – one of which is the command to love our neighbors. Christian humility engenders charity.

Let us turn now to a second version of the scenario. In this version, the humans know that there is no perfect being in charge of their fates. Rather, they know that they have been scattered at random onto the surface of the planet, the nature of which itself was fixed by mindless forces. The type of terrain that any individual human lands in is entirely a matter of chance. There is no perfect being who is in charge of the situation or who has issued any commands to the humans. They are on their own. This scenario is relevantly like the situation in which we find ourselves in a naturalistic universe. As before, I would like to focus on this question: What obligations, if any, do the better-off among these humans have to the worse-off?

I think that in this second scenario, the better-off have an obligation to assist the worse-off at least to some degree, despite not having been issued a divine command to do so. Suppose a human who has happened to land in a lush and bountiful forest happens to observe another human who has landed nearby in a dry and barren desert. The first human, if sufficiently reflective, will observe that the two have ended up where they are as a consequence of forces outside of their control. "I have happened to land in a bountiful forest, whereas this fellow has happened to land in a barren desert. We are both human and neither of us has chosen our fate. There is no higher power in charge of this situation, and it appears that if I do not help this fellow, no one else will." These are the sorts of thoughts that ought to go through the mind of the more fortunate human, who should reasonably arrive at the conclusion that the privileged have an obligation to help the less fortunate. This obligation is grounded not in any divine command but instead in the particulars of the situation. Among the more salient features of the situation is the *lack of control* the two have over their respective fates. If the winds had blown slightly differently, their situations could have been reversed. Is it not clear that it is not morally permissible to refuse entirely to offer any help to the less fortunate who find themselves in difficult circumstances through no fault of their own and who will probably suffer and even perish if we do not help them?

If this is right, then we can see that naturalistic humility, like Christian humility, leads to charity. As I suggested in the Section 4.3, naturalistic humility involves a recognition of the tremendous contribution of blind chance to the fates of human beings, and it is precisely such a recognition that should lead us to acknowledge an obligation to assist the less fortunate among us. There is plenty of room for debate here about the precise extent to which our situation in a naturalistic universe resembles the situation of the humans in the forest-or-desert scenario and about the precise extent of our obligation to assist the less fortunate, but it seems clear enough that we have some such obligation.[47] If God is dead, we have not been divinely commanded to help our fellow human beings. Nevertheless, we have such an obligation, though it is derived from a different source. And, in both a Christian universe and a naturalistic universe, the appropriate type of humility will lead us to recognize this obligation.

4.5 HOPE AND HEROISM

In "A Free Man's Worship," Bertrand Russell writes:

> That man is the product of causes which had no prevision of the end they were achieving, that his origin, his growth, his hopes and fears, his loves and his beliefs, are but the outcome of accidental collocations of atoms; that no fire, no heroism, no intensity of thought and feeling, can preserve an individual life beyond the grave; that all the labors of the ages, all the devotion, all the noonday brightness of human genius, are destined to extinction in the vast death of the solar system, and that the whole temple of man's achievement must inevitably be buried beneath the debris of a universe in ruins – all these things, if not quite beyond dispute, are yet so nearly certain that no philosophy which rejects them can hope to stand. Only within the scaffolding of these truths, only on the firm foundation of unyielding despair, can the soul's habitation henceforth be safely built.[48]

The passage is remarkable for its succinct and striking statement of naturalism, together with the suggestion (which I must confess to finding darkly hilarious) that the proper response to the truth of naturalism is *unyielding despair*. But is this correct? The third of Kant's famous three questions from the *Critique of Pure Reason* is: What may I hope? Specifically, what is it reasonable for someone who knows naturalism to be true to hope for? Indeed, if naturalism is known to be true, is there any place for hope at all, or is utter despair the only reasonable response?

Thomas Aquinas writes that "the act of hope consists in looking forward to future happiness from God."[49] Obviously there is no place for this sort of hope for those who know naturalism to be true. Although Russell's "unyielding despair" passage might lead one to think that his view is that complete despair is the appropriate attitude for the naturalist, this is not the case. Russell holds that many of us may at least reasonably hope for good lives, even in a universe of the sort he takes ours to be. According to Russell, a good life is "one inspired by love and guided by knowledge."[50] And one important piece of knowledge is the knowledge that naturalism is true. Knowledge of the truth of naturalism can, according to Russell, contribute to a good life.

But how? How should we feel, and what should we do, in light of this knowledge? Russell's answer, in a nutshell, is that we ought to face the facts with courage. He writes that "it is fear of nature that gives rise to religion."[51] The function of belief in God is to "humanize the world of nature and to make men feel that physical forces are really their allies."[52] It is a wishful superstition, a barricade thrown up between us and the truth we are afraid to face. Now, if Russell's claim is that it is always fear that drives people to religion, the claim is false; for many people, certain religious claims are simply among the things that their parents taught them and are accepted on that basis. But Russell is surely correct that fear sometimes drives people to religion. This is the idea behind the old saying that "there are no atheists in foxholes." Mark Juergensmeyer (2000) mentions an incident that took place in 1870 in which a group of American Indians were trapped by the U.S. Cavalry and "responded by spontaneously creating a ritual of dancing and hypnotic trances known as the Ghost Dance religion."[53] So we know that at least one religion was spawned by fear.[54]

If it is fear that drives us into the clutches of religion, then it is courage that can set us free. Russell's idea is that a courageous person accepts the truth of naturalism and in so doing faces the fact that "the great world . . . is neither good nor bad, and is not concerned to make us happy or unhappy."[55] Indeed, Russell suggests that facing the truth about the universe is itself a kind of victory, a heroic act:

> When, without the bitterness of impotent rebellion, we have learned both to resign ourselves to the outward rule of Fate and to recognize that the nonhuman world is unworthy of our worship, it becomes possible at last so to transform and refashion the unconscious universe, so to transmute it in the crucible of imagination, that a new image of shining gold replaces the old idol of clay.... To take into the inmost shrine of the soul the irresistible forces whose puppets we seem to be – death and change, the irrevocableness of the past, and the powerlessness of man before the blind hurry of the universe from vanity to vanity – *to feel these things and know them is to conquer them.*[56]

The victory of accepting naturalism consists in exerting control over one's own mind. In a universe in which human beings are largely at the mercy of morally indifferent forces beyond their control, one prominent kind of achievement is *taking control*. In the particular case of accepting naturalism, the victory is over fear. The religious believer is driven by fear; in this way, the believer's mind is subject to forces beyond personal control just as much as is the body. But the naturalist takes control of the mind and refuses to be ruled by fear; this victory over the universe is a worthwhile achievement in and of itself.

Interestingly, the sort of control that Russell admires corresponds closely to what the great Christian apologist C. S. Lewis identifies as one type of faith:

> Faith ... is the art of holding on to things your reason has once accepted, in spite of your changing moods. For moods will change, whatever view your reason takes.... Now that I am a Christian I do have moods in which the whole thing looks very improbable: but when I was an atheist I had moods in which Christianity looked terribly probable. The rebellion of your moods against your real self is going to come anyway. That is why Faith is such a necessary virtue: unless you teach your moods 'where they get off', you can never be either a sound Christian or even a sound atheist, but just a creature dithering to and fro, with its beliefs really dependent on the weather and the state of its digestion.[57]

Notice that Lewis speaks of the "rebellion" of moods and, toward the end of the passage, praises faith on the grounds that it decreases one's dependence on factors beyond one's control – specifically, weather and digestion. Russell and Lewis agree in praising as a virtue the ability to regulate one's beliefs in accordance with reason, and not to let one's beliefs be controlled by passions and changing moods. What they disagree about is whether reason points us toward theism or atheism. But it seems clear from this "rebellious mood" passage that Lewis would agree that *if reason told us that atheism were true*, then persistent acceptance of it would be indicative of virtue – the virtue that Russell identifies as courage and Lewis identifies as faith. Perhaps there is such a thing as naturalistic faith?

Suppose that we can hope for the sort of victory Russell envisions. A reasonable question is: Is that *all* we can hope for? To see what more we can hope for in a naturalistic universe we must delve a bit deeper. Naturalism has dark implications – implications that must be examined more fully before we can decide how much we should hope and how much we should despair in a naturalistic universe.

In *Facing Evil*, John Kekes (1990) identifies three essential conditions of human life, three unavoidable features of the human condition. The first of these is one that I have emphasized already, that "human life is vulnerable to *contingency*. . . . There are vast areas of our lives in which we lack understanding and control."[58] The second condition is the "*indifference* of the scheme of things toward human merit. There is no cosmic justice. . . . The order of nature is not a moral order. . . . It is indifferent."[59] This second condition is incompatible with, for instance, the notion that there is a divine guarantee of perfect justice. It is these first two conditions of human life that play an important role in Russell's position. The third condition (which Kekes illustrates by way of the character Kurtz from Conrad's *The Heart of Darkness*), is "the presence of destructiveness in human motivation."[60] It is important to note that Kekes takes this to be an *inevitable* feature of human nature.[61]

Of these three conditions, the second is by far the most troubling. In Graham Hess's speech from the film *Signs* that I quoted at the very beginning of this book, what distinguishes the two groups into

119

which Hess says all people can be divided is their stance with respect to Kekes's second condition. Hess says that people in the first group believe that whatever happens, "there is someone up there, watching out for them," whereas people in the second group believe that they are on their own. Hess says the people in the first group are filled with hope, and the people in the second group are filled with fear.

The idea that the universe is fundamentally reasonable and moral is a conviction that is widely held among thinkers of a variety of religious orientations. The notion of a rational and moral universe pervades ancient Greek philosophy. Heraclitus and Parmenides both sought to understand the *logos*, the rational pattern of the universe, though they disagreed about the nature of that *logos*.[62] Anaximander suggested that the Earth was in the center of the universe because there was no good reason for it to be anywhere else.[63] On trial for his life, accused by Anytus and Meletus of sophistry, atheism, and corrupting the youth of Athens, Socrates offered the following line of reasoning: "Be sure that if you put me to death ... you will do yourselves more harm than me. Meletus and Anytus can do me no harm: that is impossible, for *I am sure it is not allowed* that a good man be injured by a worse."[64] In the first book of the *Nicomachean Ethics*, Aristotle appeals to the premise that "in the realm of nature, things are naturally arranged in the best way possible."[65] The seventeenth-century philosopher Leibniz (1985) is known for holding a particularly strong version of this idea. He maintained that since this world (by which he meant all existing things throughout all of time) was created by a perfect God, it must be the best of all possible worlds.[66] We have already briefly considered a contemporary twist on this idea. At the end of Chapter 2 I mentioned John Leslie's suggestion that a personal God exists because of the presence of certain ethical requirements in the universe.[67] Writing on Ghana's independence from Britain in 1957, Martin Luther King, Jr., (1998) saw the event as "fit testimony to the fact that eventually the forces of justice triumph in the universe, and somehow the universe itself is on the side of freedom and justice."[68] The view that the universe is fundamentally rational and moral is, of course, held not only by philosophers; it is often expressed in terms of the widely held conviction that "things happen for a reason."[69]

In my first chapter I mentioned Aristotle's view that the best kind of human life is the life of the successful philosopher – a life of theoretical contemplation. I have found that one of the first objections students propose to this view is that it implies that most people cannot live the best kind of human life. Students sometimes characterize Aristotle's view as "unfair" or "elitist." I have heard this sort of objection defended by theists, agnostics, and atheists like. The objection may be stated this way:

1. If Aristotle's view is true, then most people cannot live the best kind of life.
2. But it's not true that most people cannot live the best kind of life.
3. Therefore, Aristotle's view is false.

But what on earth is the support for the second premise? My suspicion is that the students who pose this objection are motivated by the sense that *the universe just can't work that way*. And this sense is based on the notion that the universe is fundamentally rational and moral.

To begin to see just how terrifying the rejection of the idea that the universe is rational and moral is, notice that two of Kekes's three essential conditions of human life – contingency and destructiveness in human motivation – are components of the Christian view of the universe. This is clear from our earlier discussion of the Fall of Man. Humans were dependent upon God prior to the Fall; after the Fall, their dependence only increased. And part of the Christian view is that among the consequences of the Fall is the moral corruption of human nature, one manifestation of which is destructiveness in our motivation. Because of the Fall, a heart of darkness resides within each of us.

But Christianity utterly rejects the moral indifference of the universe. And it is this, I believe, that makes the Christian message fundamentally one of hope. Notice how less threatening the other two conditions are if they are combined with the other aspects of

Christianity. Yes, there are many things that are not under our control – but those things are ultimately under the control of a perfectly good God. Yes, there is a heart of darkness inside each of us – but this need not be a permanent condition. With God's help, we can overcome and eventually rid ourselves of the evil within – if not in this life, then in what comes after.

Take away this moral universe guided by a rational, perfectly powerful, wise, good creator and replace it with a mindless, indifferent, uncaring, largely uncontrollable *thing*, and these two conditions are much more threatening. There is no assurance that the evil within can be overcome – ever. The things that are not under our control are not under the control of a perfectly good being, either. Instead, they are under the control of *no being at all*.

The difference of opinion with respect to Kekes's second condition is, I think, one of the most important differences between theism and atheism. One of the reasons that George Mavrodes's moral argument for the existence of God (discussed in Section 3.5) is so unconvincing is that Mavrodes takes as a premise the claim that the universe is fundamentally just, without offering any argument for it. But since this is one of the main things that is at issue in the debate between the theist and the atheist, the atheist is unlikely to find this sort of argument compelling.

This area of disagreement is also one reason, though surely not the only one, why theists and atheists may feel tremendous animosity toward each other. The atheist affirms that there is no particular reason to think that anyone's suffering or loss makes sense, including suffering and loss experienced by theists. On the other hand, the atheist may feel that in holding that personal suffering and the deaths of loved ones do ultimately make sense, the theist is failing to appreciate fully just how bad they are. The atheist may feel particular irritation toward the theist whose faith wobbles only after a *personal* tragedy.

In many science fiction stories there comes a moment when one of the main characters is revealed to be a robot. Imagine making such a discovery about someone you love. I think that this thought experiment can convey something of what it is like to move from rejection to acceptance of Kekes's second condition. Both experiences, I suspect, involve a gut-wrenching shock of realization: Instead of something that cares, is rational, and is somewhat like us, we find something that doesn't give a damn, is indifferent to reason, and is completely alien. Some readers might find Socrates' insistence that the vicious aren't allowed to harm the virtuous or my students' insistence that the universe just can't work that way quaint or naïve – but I suspect a little reflection will reveal a tendency toward this sort of reasoning in all of us. One of the implications of the truth of Kekes's second condition is that there is *nothing* so bad or so unfair that it could not happen simply because it would be too evil or too unjust. And yet do we not find within ourselves the susceptibility to disbelieve some things on precisely such grounds? How natural is it for us to think that such-and-such just can't be true – it would be too awful! But if we know naturalism to be true, it is never reasonable to employ this sort of reasoning.[70] That such-and-such would be the worst imaginable thing that could happen to you, or that could happen to the human race, is of absolutely no interest to the Powers That Be in a naturalistic universe. It constitutes not even the slightest basis for thinking that such-and-such will not occur.

In the 1984 film *Terminator*, heroine Sarah Connor finds herself the target of a robot whose sole purpose is to kill her. Desperate to get her to understand the gravity of her situation, Reese, who has been sent to save Sarah from the Terminator, gives her the following minilecture: "Listen. Understand. That Terminator is out there. It can't be reasoned with; it can't be bargained with; it doesn't feel pity or remorse or fear; and it absolutely will not stop. Ever. Until you are dead."[71] If we substitute "The Universe" for "That Terminator," then this speech summarizes one of the most significant things we learn when we learn that naturalism is true. Of course, unlike the Terminator, the naturalistic universe does not *intend* to destroy you. But although it is not out to get you, get you it eventually will.

There is surely a place for fear and at least temporary despair in the face of this bit of information about the universe. I think Russell is correct in suggesting that the naturalist ought to strive to conquer this fear, and that doing so is something of an accomplishment. I think Russell is also right in suggesting that at least some of us may hope for lives that are worth living, even in a naturalistic universe. But these points suggest further questions. For example, supposing we can conquer our fear and accept naturalism, what should be our long-term attitude toward Kekes's three conditions – particularly the second one? And of course there is the difficult question of *how* to go about securing a good life in a naturalistic universe. I would like to propose an answer to the first question and make a modest suggestion about the second.

As a long-term response to the three essential conditions of human life, Kekes proposes that we adopt what he calls "the reflective temper." This reflective temper has both cognitive and emotional components. The cognitive component consists of what Kekes calls an "enlarged understanding," which is the persistent acceptance of the three essential conditions of human life. These must be accepted fully and unwaveringly in much the way Russell suggests. They must not just be accepted and forgotten about or shoved to the back of one's mind; they should be held before the mind and reflected upon regularly.[72] Above all, the person with the reflective temper avoids what Kekes calls "the transcendental temptation," which is to "suppose that behind what appear to be the essential conditions of life there is a deeper order that is favorable to humanity."[73]

The main benefit of the reflective temper, according to Kekes, is that "it increases our control."[74] Specifically, "[W]hat we learn to control is *ourselves*, both as victims and as agents of evil."[75] Like Russell, Kekes highlights the significance of getting control over ourselves. Among the ways that the reflective temper increases our control over ourselves are that it "keeps our expectations realistic" and it helps us "to accommodate failures we could not avoid, by preparing us for them."[76] Kekes's points here are relatively straightforward: By having an accurate understanding of what the universe is like, we protect ourselves from inflated expectations and disillusionment. Losing one's faith can be traumatic; the trauma can be avoided if we are not so foolish as to have faith in the first place. Kekes writes: "Unrealistic expectations are more likely to be disappointed than realistic ones. And their disappointment is likely to be much more damaging for those who are unprepared for it than for those who understand their own vulnerability."[77]

As an illustration of the sort of thing Kekes has in mind, consider the method recommended by de Montaigne (1966) in his essay "That to Philosophize is to Learn to Die." As the title suggests, de Montaigne is concerned specifically with death. He is looking for a way of preparing people for both their own demise and the demise of their loved ones so that they will not suffer the negative emotional consequences so often associated with death. He writes:

> They go, they come, they trot, they dance – of death no news. All that is fine. But when it comes, either to them or to their wives, children, or friends, surprising them unprepared and defenseless, what torments, what cries, what frenzy, what despair overwhelms them! . . . If it were an enemy we could avoid, I would advise us to borrow the arms of cowardice. But since that cannot be, since it catches you just the same, whether you flee like a coward or act like a man . . . let us learn to meet it steadfastly and to combat it. And to begin to strip it of its greatest advantage against us. . . . Let us rid it of its strangeness, come to know it, get used to it. Let us have nothing on our minds as often as death. At every moment let us picture it in our imagination in all its aspects. . . . Thus did the great Egyptians, who, in the midst of their feasts and their greatest pleasures, had the skeleton of a dead man brought before them, to serve as a reminder to the guests.[78]

De Montaigne's idea is that by keeping the prospect of death steadily before us, we will acquire increased control over our own emotions. In particular, we will be freed from fear of death. The trick is to be aware that death can strike anyone at any time. If one keeps this in mind at all times, then one will never be surprised by death. De Montaigne suggests that "[k]nowing how to die frees us from all subjection and constraint."[79]

If Russell is right that it is fear that typically drives people to religion, and if the main object of fear is death, then perhaps we can use de Montaigne's method to free ourselves from the fear of death, to avoid the transcendental temptation, and to achieve the glorious victory that Russell praises in his passages. Whether all of this is so I leave to the reader to determine.[80]

Kekes makes another suggestion about how the reflective temper can be beneficial. This suggestion relates specifically to the third of the three essential conditions, the heart of darkness within us. The suggestion is that we should be aware that we have destructive tendencies within us and to be on the lookout for them. The point of this is that "we can become aware, through reflection, of our various dispositions to cause evil and, as a result, change our conduct."[81] This is an area where science can be of assistance. For example, Steven Pinker writes:

> In social psychology experiments, people consistently overrate their own skill, honesty, generosity, and autonomy. They overestimate their contribution to a joint effort, chalk up their successes to skill and their failures to luck, and always feel that the other side has gotten the better deal in a compromise. People keep up these self-serving illusions even when they are wired to what they think is an accurate lie–detector. This shows that they are not lying to the experimenter but lying to themselves.[82]

Recognizing that our minds have a tendency to bias certain kinds of information in our favor allows us to be on the lookout for and correct for this bias. Just as knowing that a scale always reads five pounds heavy enables us to use it to discover our actual weight, knowing that our mind tends to slant the data in certain ways enables us to get closer to the truth by taking the slant into account. And this can help to avoid disagreements and conflict that can result from widespread bias of the sort Pinker describes.

Combining the suggestions of Russell and Kekes, then, I propose that the naturalist's self-concept ought to be as a hero, struggling to satisfy the demands of morality and secure a life of internal meaning for the individual and for loved ones in a universe which is at best utterly indifferent and at worst downright hostile to both projects. The naturalist is a hero who must pursue worthwhile projects with the understanding that "they are vulnerable to evil no matter how hard and well [I try] to succeed at them."[83] Victory can be at best temporary, but it is a victory worth struggling for. As Russell observes, "[H]appiness is nonetheless true happiness because it must come to an end, nor do thought and love lose their value because they are not everlasting."[84] And, as Kekes suggests, the naturalist must keep these fundamental facts about the universe in mind as much as possible.

Part of the Christian conception of the universe is the idea that human beings are involved in a *cosmic war*. Some of the main components of the backdrop of this struggle as it is conceived in traditional Christianity were described in the earlier discussion of the Fall of Man. It is a struggle of individuals against themselves. As C. S. Lewis puts it, "[W]e are not merely imperfect creatures who must be improved: we are . . . rebels who must put down our arms."[85] According to traditional Christianity, moreover, much of history is to be understood in terms of this struggle. Gordon Graham suggests that we ought to view history as "a cosmic battle between forces of light and forces of darkness, one in which human beings are left free to make a choice about which side they will join."[86]

In place of this vision of oneself as a soldier in a war between good and evil, I suggest that naturalists view themselves as engaged in a struggle against a wild animal. The struggle is not on a battlefield where conflict rages between the forces of dark and light and where victory and salvation are assured only for the right side. Rather, the struggle is to tame an uncaring, irrational beast, and success is anything but certain; everyone has something of the beast inside and an important part of the struggle is conquering this inner monster. The inexorable, uncaring laws of nature are the arena, and as much as possible they must be understood and put to use. Within the combatants are destructive emotional tendencies that arose not as a consequence of the Fall, but rather of the slow, mindless working of the evolutionary forces that shaped the human mind. This inner struggle and the prospects for victory in it are the topics of Section 4.6.

4.6 MORAL EDUCATION AND SCIENCE

Evident in many Platonic dialogues is a concern with finding a reliable method of producing virtuous adults. In Plato's mind virtuous people are more valuable than gold, as the following remark by Socrates in the *Meno* makes clear:

> [I]f the good were so by nature, we would have people who knew which among the young were by nature good; we would take those whom they had pointed out and guard them in the Acropolis, sealing them up there much more carefully than gold so that no one could corrupt them, and when they reached maturity they would be useful to their cities.[87]

Why are virtuous people so important to Plato? The answer is that they are the key to lasting human happiness. Plato thought that lasting happiness is possible only within a just society, and a just society is one in which a small group of virtuous rulers have control over the masses. Plato saw democracy as an inferior, degenerate form of government. In his masterpiece *Republic* Plato tried to lay out in detail the workings of a perfectly just society, one in which lasting human happiness would be guaranteed. The dialogue includes instructions for how to raise and educate the rulers of this ideal society (the philosopher–kings). The following words from Socrates indicate the importance of these rulers in Plato's scheme:

> Until philosophers rule as kings or those who are now called kings and leading men genuinely and adequately philosophize, that is, until political power and philosophy entirely coincide, while the many natures who at present pursue either one exclusively are forcibly prevented from doing so, cities will have no rest from evils . . . nor, I think, will the human race.[88]

This explains why finding a *reliable* method for producing virtuous persons is so important. What is required to guarantee lasting human happiness is a steady supply of virtuous replacements for old rulers when they step down or pass away. At my university, as at many universities in the United States, there has been a recent surge of interest in the topic of moral education. This interest seems to have been triggered in part by the terrorist attacks of September 11, 2001, but perhaps more directly by the recent spate of destructive corporate scandals, the most notorious of which involve business giants Enron and WorldCom. This tells us something about who has the power in our society. What *we* need, it seems, is not virtuous *kings* but virtuous *CEOs*.

In a naturalistic universe, there is no divine guarantee of perfect justice, and the extent to which self-interest and the demands of morality coincide is a contingent matter.[89] While it is next to certain that a perfect coincidence between the two will never be achieved, greater and lesser approximations of this ideal are possible. As humans are social animals, *just societies* are essential for getting as close to the ideal as is humanly possible. As Kekes puts it, the ideal state is one in which "the question of why one should be moral has the obvious answer that living morally is the best way of living."[90] And, as Plato realized, an essential element of a just society is control by the virtuous. This does not mean that we must follow Plato in rejecting democracy. In a democracy, the people have the power; consequently, if a democratic society is to be a just society, the people must be virtuous. Finding a reliable way of producing virtuous citizens would be one of the greatest breakthroughs in the history of humankind; it would be a breakthrough that would improve every society, regardless of its system of government.

If naturalism is true, then human beings are part of the natural world and consequently can be understood using the methods of science. One benefit of abandoning the myth of a nonphysical soul that is the "true self" and that is responsible for our mental activity is an increased understanding of how the brain works and how it is responsible for our mental states. In a naturalistic universe, it is a person's physical states, particularly the states of the brain and nervous system, that are responsible for mental activity and, therefore, for character as well. Advances in science have given us the ability (though not all take advantage of it) to make ourselves physically healthier than ever before. We have the knowledge and the technology to live longer and healthier lives than at any point in human history. In a naturalistic universe, it makes sense to put science, particularly neuroscience, to work in the service of the ancient Platonic task of finding a reliable method of making people virtuous. Russell made a proposal along these lines in 1925. He was concerned specifically with the task of making people more courageous. He suggested that science might have an important role to play in this task and he made the following remark: "Perhaps the physiological sources of courage could be discovered by comparing the blood of a cat with that of a rabbit."[91] It is hard to tell how seriously Russell intended his remark to be taken, but tremendous progress in understanding the neurological underpinnings of fear has been made since he said it, and, in fact, scientists have successfully bred unusually courageous rats.[92] Although matters are far more complicated than Russell's remark suggests, the suggestion that we try to use science as a means to moral improvement is one that should be taken seriously.

This sort of proposal will undoubtedly conjure up in the minds of many readers the horrific spectacle of moral education through science found in Aldous Huxley's (1998) classic novel *Brave New World*. The novel depicts a society in which every citizen is assigned one particular role, and through a combination of genetic engineering, conditioning, and "hypnopadia", or sleep-teaching, each citizen is shaped physically, mentally, and morally to fit that role. The purpose of all of this is to ensure social stability. Of particular importance is that the citizens avoid experiencing intense emotions; one of the slogans indoctrinated into every citizen is, "[W]hen the individual feels, the community reels."[93] As a means to this end, emotional attachment to specific human beings is prohibited as it is exactly this sort of attachment that leads to intense emotions and social strife. As one of the Controllers (the small elite group of rulers) puts it:

> Mother, monogamy, romance. High spurts the fountain; fierce and foamy the wild jet. The urge has but a single outlet. My love, my baby. No wonder these poor pre–moderns were made wicked and miserable. Their world didn't allow them to take things easily, didn't allow them to be sane, virtuous, happy . . . they were forced to feel strongly . . . how could they be stable?[94]

In this brave new world, everyone is like the modified Sisyphus Richard Taylor envisioned in the final chapter of his *Good and Evil*: All citizens *want* to do the tasks assigned to them. Every citizen has been conditioned to *love* doing what society needs. As Huxley's Director of Hatcheries explains, "That is the secret of happiness and virtue – liking what you've got to do."[95] A particularly humorous illustration of this is the reaction of an elevator operator upon arriving at the roof: "He flung open the gates. The warm glory of the afternoon sunlight made him start and blink his eyes. 'Oh, roof!' he repeated in a voice of rapture. He was as though suddenly and joyfully awakened from a dark annihilating stupor. 'Roof!'"[96] This is a society in which the demands of "morality" (such as they are) and "happiness" (such as it is) do indeed coincide. But "happiness" means gentle, childish pleasure. The virtuous citizen in the brave new world is in fact a self-indulgent child; delayed gratification is condemned rather than commended.

I think that what is horrifying about the moral education in the brave new world is not primarily the *means* through which the morality is imposed but rather the *content* of that morality. It is a moral system that should horrify us because it precludes some of the greatest goods in human life, including meaningful personal relationships and intellectual and artistic achievement. One problem with the method described in Huxley's novel is that it is a method that does not produce genuinely virtuous persons. It is a method that produces spoiled children.[97]

A second problematic feature of the moral education portrayed in the novel is that it is imposed by the state. In my view, governments are not, in general, to be trusted, and so I think that giving any government the power to shape the character of its citizens (should this become possible) would be a tremendous mistake. The potential abuses are both obvious and great.

What, then, do I have in mind when I suggest that science be put to use in the service of moral improvement? I lack the scientific knowledge to make anything like a detailed proposal; what I hope to offer instead is a proposal about the direction future research might take. My suggestion will be rooted in various philosophical assumptions – many of which I have already identified – and is best understood as a conditional claim of the following form: If the philosophical assumptions in question are correct, then the kind of research I will suggest is a good idea.

Aristotle and Kant, arguably the two most influential ethical philosophers in the history of Western philosophy, disagree about many things, but they are united by their acceptance of the following claim: Becoming a morally good person is a struggle. It is a struggle between practical reason (the capacity to think rationally about how to act) on the one hand and emotions and desires on the other. The two philosophers disagree about the precise nature of the struggle. On Aristotle's view, the conflict is between human emotions and a person's conception of the good life. This conflict is successfully resolved when one's conception of the good life is the correct one and when one's emotions are in line with this correct conception. In a fully virtuous person, the rational and appetitive parts of the soul will both function properly; hence it will be true to say that "in him everything is in harmony with the voice of reason"[98] A virtuous person's emotions, pleasures, and pains will be appropriate, beliefs about what is valuable will be true, and beliefs and emotions will track each other.

Kant's writing on moral character emphasizes a continual internal struggle to fulfill one's moral obligations. Being virtuous is largely a matter of mastering one's unruly desires for morally impermissible courses of action. Kant at one point characterizes moral virtue as "the capacity and considered resolve to withstand . . . what opposes the moral disposition in us."[99] Elsewhere, Kant is so pessimistic about the prospect of gaining the upper hand over one's unruly desires that he suggests that "[a] good example (exemplary conduct) should not serve as a model but only as a proof that it is really possible to act in conformity with duty."[100] Kant apparently takes it that overcoming the inclinations that pull us away from doing our duty is so difficult that proof that it is even possible is required! Kant sets a somewhat less demanding criterion for victory in the struggle between reason and passion than Aristotle did. Kant says: "[V]irtue contains a positive command to a human being, namely to bring all his capacities and inclinations under his (reason's) control and so to rule over himself."[101] On Kant's view one's emotions need not be in complete harmony with the voice of reason; all that is required is that one master one's emotions to the extent that they do not prevent one from fulfilling one's moral obligations.

When reason is not victorious in this struggle, the result is the all-too-common phenomenon that philosophers call "weakness of will." One of the most well-known descriptions of this phenomenon comes from the Apostle Paul: "I can will what is right, but I cannot do it. For I do not do the good I want, but the evil I do not want is what I do."[102] The neuroscientist Joseph LeDoux (1996), in his book *The Emotional Brain*, describes what may be the features of the brain that make fear-related weakness of will possible. Of particular importance are the cerebral cortex, the area of the brain that is responsible for what we intuitively think of as higher-order cognitive functions, including reasoning and voluntary action, and the amygdala, an intuitively more primitive brain structure that is heavily involved in producing various physiological changes and behaviors associated with fear. LeDoux writes:

> [I]t is well known that the connections from the cortical areas to the amygdala are far weaker than the connections from the amygdala to the cortex. This may explain why it is so easy for emotional information to invade our conscious thoughts, but so hard for us to gain conscious control over our emotions.[103]

A more scientifically knowledgeable Paul might have said: "I do not the good that my cerebral cortex wants, but the evil my amygdala wants, that I do." One possible area of scientific research, then, relates to what we might call the *weakness-of-will* problem. The human brain ought to be studied with an eye toward helping us overcome emotions that are at odds with our considered judgments about what is right and good. One reason that this approach seems somewhat promising is that it would seem to be continuous with research that is already underway. The quest to understand and control certain negative emotions – like the feelings of depression, anxiety, and fear – is already in progress. Another contemporary neuroscientist, Antonio

Damasio (2003), is optimistic about the impact advances in neuroscience will have on this quest:

> Within the next two decades, perhaps sooner, the neurobiology of emotion and feelings will allow biomedical science to develop effective treatments for pain and depression grounded on a sweeping understanding of how genes are expressed in particular brain regions and how these regions cooperate to make us emote and feel.... Combined with psychological interventions, the new therapies will revolutionize mental health. The treatments available today will appear by then as gross and archaic as surgery without anesthesia appears to us now.[104]

My suggestion is that the catalog of emotions under study be expanded to include hatred, jealousy, and lust, to name a few. The goal is not the elimination of these emotions altogether but rather an increased ability to control them. Researchers seeking to understand the brain chemistry involved in depression are not trying to develop a drug that will eliminate the emotion of sadness altogether; instead, they are trying to give patients increased control over their feelings of sadness, anxiety, and hopelessness. The idea of a strength-of-will pill may seem ludicrous, and I do not mean to suggest that such a thing is around the corner – but certain products designed to help smokers control their desire for cigarettes (the nicotine patch, for example) are in the same family as this hypothetical drug.

In the final section of *The Emotional Brain*, LeDoux speculates on how the human brain might be shaped by evolution in the future. On the basis of the observation that "the cortical connections with the amygdala are far greater in primates than in other mammals," LeDoux speculates that the cortex-to-amygdala connections in humans may gradually increase over time and that "the cortex might gain more and more control over the amygdala, possibly allowing future humans to be able to better control their emotions."[105] These hypothetical beings would achieve Kantian virtue much more easily than we do because of the way their brains are wired. LeDoux describes another alternative:

> Yet, there is another possibility. The increased connectivity between the amygdala and the cortex involves fibers going from the cortex to the amygdala as well as from the amygdala to the cortex. If these

nerve pathways strike a balance, it is possible that the struggle between thought and emotion may ultimately be resolved not by the
dominance of emotional centers by cortical cognitions, but by a more
harmonious integration of reason and passion. With increased connec-
tivity between the cortex and the amygdala, cognition and emotion
might begin to work together rather than separately.[106]

This other possibility corresponds not with Kantian virtue but rather
with Aristotelian virtue. LeDoux's hope of a "harmonious integration
of reason and passion" is reminiscent of Aristotle's suggestion that
in the virtuous person, "everything is in harmony with the voice of
reason."[107] LeDoux's speculation suggests that over time the wiring
of the human brain will change in such a way that people will naturally be much closer to either the Kantian or the Aristotelian ethical
ideal than they are now. Perhaps evolution will eliminate weakness
of will if it is given enough time. But why wait? Nearly two and a half
millennia after Aristotle noted the conflict between the rational and
appetitive parts of the soul, we are uncovering the brain structures
responsible for this aspect of human nature. Perhaps a way could be
found to increase the connections between the cortex and the amygdala artificially. Obviously such an endeavor is far off and should be
undertaken cautiously, but the more we learn about the brain, the
more feasible the project seems.

The brain modification I am imagining here would be a relatively
direct way of defeating weakness of will. As things currently stand,
we have only more indirect methods for dealing with weakness of
will. One of these indirect ways can be culled from Kant's discussion of the role of sympathy in the psychology of a virtuous person.
Drawing out this method will require a brief foray into Kantian ex-
egesis. Readers with an interest in Kant's views on moral character
may find this digression interesting; others may wish to skip to its
conclusion a few pages hence. Kant writes:

> Sympathetic joy and sadness...are sensible feelings of pleasure or
> displeasure...at another's state of joy or pain. Nature has already
> implanted in human beings receptivity to these feelings. But to use this
> as a means to promoting active and rational benevolence is still...a
> duty.[108]

The passage suggests that feelings of sympathy have a role to play in the psychology of a virtuous person. But what exactly is this role in Kant's view? Kant is notorious for denigrating the emotions and for giving what he calls "the motive of duty" a central place in his account of what motivates a virtuous person. Acting from the motive of duty clearly involves performing an action because one is obligated to do so, but much ink has been spilled in trying to decide exactly how central this type of motivation must be in the Kantian virtuous agent.[109] We can start to shed some light on this issue by noticing that Kant suggests that sympathetic feelings are to be used as a *means* to "active and rational benevolence." A bit later, Kant says that the tendency to have feelings of sympathy "is still one of the impulses that nature has implanted in us to do what the representation of duty alone might not accomplish."[110] How are we to understand these claims? One possibility is that Kant's idea is that sympathetic feelings can provide an extra bit of motivation to do one's duty in cases where the motive of duty alone would be insufficient. While this is surely true, it seems unlikely that Kant would commend sympathetic feelings for their role in providing an extra motivational boost. Consider, for example, this passage from *Religion Within the Limits of Reason Alone*:

> [T]he impurity of the human heart consists in this, that although the maxim is indeed good in respect of its object...and perhaps even strong enough for practice, it is yet not purely moral; that is, it has not, as it should have, adopted the law *alone* as its *all-sufficient* incentive: instead, it usually (perhaps, every time) stands in need of other incentives beyond this, in determining the will to do what duty demands.[111]

In this passage Kant suggests that the need to rely on motives other than the motive of duty indicates a kind of moral weakness. A fully virtuous person would not *need* to be motivated by feelings of sympathy to help his fellow man; the recognition that he is morally obligated to do so would be sufficient by itself to motivate him. In Kant's view, feelings of sympathy as motives would be at best a temporary crutch to be used on the path to genuine virtue and would be superfluous as motives once genuine virtue was attained. But why, then, does everyone – including a fully virtuous person – have an obligation to cultivate such feelings?

The following remark from Kant's *Lectures on Ethics* suggests an answer to this question: "[T]he function of the sensuous motives should be merely that of overcoming greater sensuous obstacles so that understanding can again bear rule."[112] An example of the sort of thing that I believe Kant has in mind here happened to me while I was puzzling over this issue in connection with my doctoral dissertation. I was in the midst of working on the dissertation in the dead of winter in northern Indiana when an acquaintance of mine called on the telephone. The battery in his car was dead and he asked me to drive over and help him jump-start his car. Initially, I was inclined to refuse out of selfish motives: I wanted to finish working on the dissertation in order to finish a certain section of it that day. But after a couple of moments, feelings of sympathy welled up inside me. I was pained at the thought of the poor fellow having to walk home alone in the cold. One plausible way of understanding what happened next illustrates Kant's suggestion in the passage just cited. The feeling of sympathy weakened my desire to continue working on the dissertation. My desire was not so much overridden as it was snuffed out of existence. Thus, when I did in fact act, my recognition that I ought to help the fellow out was sufficient by itself to overcome my (weakened) desire to continue working, and hence to motivate me to do my duty. In the war between reason and the emotions, some emotions can serve the cause of reason. They are to be commended not primarily as motives but rather for their role in weakening the emotions that threaten to yank us from the path of duty.[113]

In my view, what is required for Kantian virtue is not that the motive of duty be the *only* thing that motivates a virtuous person to do his or her duty, but that it be a *sufficient* motive in the following counterfactual sense: Even if no other supporting motive had been present at the time of action, the person would have done his or her duty anyway. The motive of duty would have been sufficient, by itself, to overcome any conflicting motives the agent in fact had on the occasion in question. This is the mark of virtue.

With this background in place, it is easy to make sense of Kant's description of one method for avoiding weakness of will. Kant writes:

> It is therefore a duty not to avoid the places where the poor who lack the most basic necessities are to be found but rather to seek them out, and not to shun sickrooms or debtors' prisons and so forth in order to avoid sharing painful feelings one may not be able to resist.[114]

Kant's idea is that we ought to seek out places where human suffering is to be found in order to strengthen our tendency to feel sympathy for the suffering of others. Feelings of sympathy are useful for weakening desires that incline us away from the demands of morality. This is a relatively indirect method of defeating at least some types of weakness of will: Strengthen your feelings of sympathy and these will help reason to win the battle against emotions inclining you toward callousness. But what if science could provide us with a more direct and reliable way of weakening or gaining control over these kinds of emotions? Amputating an infected limb is one way of preventing the patient from dying of infection – but science has shown us a less crude way of accomplishing the same goal through the use of penicillin. Similarly, science has given us better ways of diminishing feelings of depression and the desire for cigarettes. Perhaps, then, it could give us better ways of diminishing or controlling fear, hatred, cowardice, and lust as well. The type of brain modification inspired by LeDoux's remarks might be one such way.

Of course, even if this sort of project could be perfected, it would not by itself provide us with a reliable way of making people virtuous. This is due in part to the fact that there is more to being good than being strong-willed. Ethical knowledge, for instance, is an important component of virtue. And the scientific discoveries that might result from the sort of research I am proposing would be not a replacement but a supplement to other more familiar parts of the process of moral improvement – receiving a proper upbringing, for instance. Aristotle's words are no less relevant today than they were when he wrote them over two thousand years ago: "[I]t is no small matter whether one habit or another is inculcated in us from early childhood; on the contrary, it makes a considerable difference, or, rather, all the difference."[115]

My proposal that science can help us become morally better should not be confused with the "jaunty optimism" that John Cottingham rightly disparages.[116] I am confident that Kekes's three essential conditions of human life will prevent us from ever achieving a heaven on earth. But naturalism offers more grounds for hope in the sort of project I have described than do at least some versions of the Christian outlook. I observed earlier that the message of Christianity is fundamentally one of hope, but it is important to realize that what it offers primarily is hope with respect to what lies *beyond* this world. In some ways, Christianity is much less optimistic about what can be achieved *in this world* than is naturalism. At least some versions of Christianity imply that we will never be able to get very far on our own in controlling the heart of darkness within ourselves. If this dark heart is part of a punishment imposed on humanity as a consequence of the Fall of Man, then we can no more control it through science than we can use science to make ourselves immortal. God will not permit either project to succeed. In a similar vein, if C. S. Lewis is right in suggesting that God uses suffering in this world to prevent us from getting too attached to the world, or if John Hick is correct in his view that this world is primarily a "vale of soul-making," then there are definite upper limits to the extent of happiness and justice that can be achieved in this world. Naturalism, by contrast, implies that there are no such divinely imposed limits. Without God, there is no higher being to watch out for us – but neither is there such a being to keep us down. The upper limits of justice and happiness remain to be discovered.

I would like to make a point about the urgency of pursuing the ancient Platonic project. Paul Kurtz writes: "Mankind now possesses the technology to destroy itself – unless, that is, man is able to redirect by means of rational control the blind forces now threatening his existence, to seize his own destiny and become his own master."[117] One area in which science has made tremendous strides in the course of human history is weapons research. The progress we have made in discovering efficient ways of killing each other is truly mind-boggling. There are weapons currently in existence that can annihilate millions of human beings in a single instant.

I sometimes present my students with the following simple thought experiment: Imagine that every person in the world has access to a button which, if pressed, would immediately destroy the Earth, eliminating human life from the universe entirely. The question to consider is: How long would the Earth remain in existence under these circumstances? It seems clear that anyone who suggests a time frame longer than around ten seconds lacks the slightest conception of the sort of world in which we live. Indeed, it is clear that unless the buttons were distributed more or less simultaneously, the process of handing them out would be nowhere near completion before someone pressed a button.

The point of this thought experiment lies in the fact that we are progressing slowly but steadily toward this idealized situation. For most of human history, no human being had the power to initiate a war that would have a good chance of killing all life on the planet. Now some do. As weapons technology continues to advance by leaps and bounds, the ability to inflict massive destruction becomes more and more widely available. Our weapons are not only becoming more lethal; like our cellular telephones they are becoming more accessible, convenient, and compact. It is this phenomenon, in part, that allegedly led the Bush administration to initiate extensive military action after the attacks of September 11, 2001, including the controversial 2003 preemptive invasion of Iraq.[118]

Our incredible technological progress has contributed to many of the problems we currently face. But it also offers some grounds for hope. We have used science to master many of the fundamental forces at work in the external world. We ought to focus our efforts now on using science to master the heart of darkness within us. In a naturalistic universe, there is no *a priori* reason to think that such a project cannot succeed. There is no divine guarantee that such a project will fail, and there is no divine command that we ought not make the effort. Moreover, the source of the heart of darkness – the human nervous system – is part of the natural, physical world; it is not a nonphysical soul, forever inaccessible to science. In a naturalistic world, the human mind is fully a product of blind forces at work over countless eons. There is nothing sacred about its design; it is not part of a divine plan, or a divine construction that we are forbidden to manipulate. Owen Flanagan (2002) writes:

> [T]he basic emotions may well have evolved as adaptations in close ancestors or in us . . . but whether they continue to function as such depends on how tightly bound they are to certain triggers, and the differences between the environments we now live in and the ones in which these adaptations arose. Any trait, given the right kind of environmental change, can become maladaptive.[119]

In an environment in which the sweetest kind of food is fruit and protein is relatively rare, having a strong desire for sweet tastes and meat may be beneficial in the long haul. But when the environment is laden with easily accessible cakes, candies, and bacon double cheeseburgers, such strong desires produce obesity on a scale the world has never seen, together with a slew of serious health problems.[120] Similarly, in an environment in which there are strict limits to the amount of destruction that a single human being can produce, uncontrollable fear, anger, and lust may be relatively advantageous over the long haul. But as the capacity of individual humans to destroy increases as a result of advancing technology, such emotions becoming increasingly dangerous.

We have not been content with the gifts of nature that have happened to come our way. Instead, we have used science to wrestle more and more gifts away from nature. We do not walk. We use bicycles, elevators, cars, trains, subways, and airplanes. We do not live outdoors, setting our schedule according to the rising and setting of the sun. We live indoors, and we shape the availability of light to our schedule rather than the other way around. Bertrand Russell observes that "[t]eeth are not extracted as they were when [I] was young, by tying a string to them and the door handle and then shutting the door."[121] We have not allowed ourselves to be utterly at the mercy of the external forces of nature. Why should we allow ourselves to be utterly at the mercy of our own nervous system?

This nervous system, together with our rapidly increasing capacity to destroy each other, poses a serious threat. As the Controller in *Brave New World* explains, it was exactly this sort of threat that led people to accept the society that Huxley intends us to find repulsive: "What's the point of truth or beauty or knowledge when the anthrax bombs are popping all around you? That was when science first began to be controlled.... People were ready to have even their appetites controlled then. Anything for a quiet life."[122]

The citizens in *Brave New World* saved themselves by allowing themselves to be turned into children, capable only of pretend virtue and false happiness. Can we do better? Without God, there is no guarantee that we will be able to save ourselves from ourselves. But neither is there a guarantee that we will fail. There is room for *hope*. My suggestion is that we focus our efforts on the attempt.

FIVE

CREEDS TO LIVE BY

"Do not think that I have come to bring peace to the earth; I have not come to bring peace, but a sword."

– Jesus[1]

5.1 TO BELIEVE OR NOT TO BELIEVE?

Toward the end of the *Phaedo* Socrates gives a fairly detailed description of the universe that includes an account of the nature of the underworld and the fates various kinds of people face in the afterlife.[2] After giving this lengthy account and immediately prior to bathing himself in preparation for the drinking of the hemlock, Socrates makes the following remarks:

> No sensible man would insist that these things are as I have described them, but I think it is fitting for a man to risk the belief – for the risk is a noble one – that this, or something like this, is true about our souls and their dwelling places, since the soul is evidently immortal, and a man should repeat this to himself as if it were an incantation, which is why I have been prolonging my tale.[3]

This is one of the earliest passages I am aware of in which appears the idea that, while knowledge of the supernatural is beyond our capacity, we should nevertheless try to acquire certain beliefs about it. Socrates' idea seems to be that having certain beliefs about the supernatural will make us "of good cheer" during life, capable of facing death as he did, without fear, and that it will make us better people.[4]

143

A similar idea underlies Pascal's famous wager. Pascal holds that knowledge of God's existence or nonexistence is beyond the reach of human reason:

> God is, or is not. But towards which side will we lean? Reason cannot decide anything. There is an infinite chaos separating us. At the far end of this infinite distance a game is being played and the coin will come down heads or tails. How will you wager? Reason cannot make you choose one way or the other, reason cannot make you defend either of the two choices.[5]

According to Pascal, the eternal happiness that one would gain if one genuinely believed in God *and* if God were to exist implies that each of us should try to inculcate in ourselves genuine belief in God – indeed, we would be fools not to – even though we cannot reason our way to God's existence. Belief in God is the only rational bet. Much more recently, John Cottingham defended a variation of Pascal's argument. In Cottingham's version, as in Socrates' version, at least some of the benefits of belief are ones we acquire in this life. Cottingham summarizes his argument this way:

> First, there are clear benefits attached to the spiritual life. Second, the metaphysical doctrines underpinning it relate to matters which are not within the domain of rational knowledge. Third, that is something that we need not worry about too much, however, since the adoption of the relevant practices will generate a passionate commitment that bypasses the need for prior rational conviction.... It makes sense to go the Pascalian route, take the risk, and gradually initiate oneself into the relevant practices, rather than remaining outside in an unsatisfied stance of dispassionate cognitive aloofness.[6]

We have already seen Kant's version of this basic idea: The reason we should try to believe in God is that doing so is the only way we can fulfill all of our moral obligations. It is important to note that these arguments, even if completely successful, in no way indicate that the supernatural doctrines in question are *true*.[7] Instead, they are intended to show that we ought to believe such doctrines, not because they are true, but for some other reason.

I want to consider a version of this idea according to which we should try to inculcate certain beliefs about the supernatural on the grounds that widespread acceptance of those beliefs will make us better off in general. Specifically, I will consider the suggestion that, assuming *reason* cannot tell us whether Christianity is true or false, we should nevertheless try to get ourselves and others to accept Christianity because doing so will make us, in general, better off in this life.

Evaluating this suggestion obviously requires examining the consequences of widespread acceptance of Christianity. Furthermore, as there are many varieties of Christianity, there is the possibility that the consequences of widespread acceptance of these differing forms may vary. A complete study of the effects of Christianity throughout history is clearly outside the scope of the present work, as is a discussion of the many forms of Christianity. Instead I will identify certain elements of thought that are clearly present in the Old Testament and argue that any version of Christianity – or any system of beliefs for that matter – that includes these elements is for that reason dangerous. Its widespread acceptance is likely to have very bad consequences for many of us. Naturalism lacks these elements and therefore is, in this respect at least, a less dangerous doctrine. I will not attempt a full comparison of the consequences of accepting naturalism versus those of accepting Christianity, nor will I attempt to determine which versions of Christianity, if any, are free of the dangerous elements I have identified. My thesis in this section, then, is this: Certain views in the Old Testament are very dangerous, and the less widely held these views are, the better off we all are.

The first of these dangerous elements is the notion that *there is a God who has selected a particular group of people to be His chosen people.* One of the most important narratives in the Old Testament is the account of how, of all the different peoples on the face of the earth, God selected one group – the Israelites – to be His chosen people. After hardening the heart of the Egyptian Pharoah in order to "show [him] my power, and to make my name resound through all the earth," God has Moses lead the Israelites out of Egypt.[8] Once the Israelites reach Mount Sinai, God tells Moses to convey a message to the rest of the Israelites: "[I]f you obey my voice and keep my covenant, you shall be my treasured possession out of all the peoples. Indeed, the whole earth is mine, but you shall be for me a priestly kingdom and a holy nation."[9]

The second dangerous element is the idea that *there is a God whose commands trump all other considerations*. Earlier, I noted the importance of obedience in the Christian scheme of things. This idea – the fact that God has commanded that a given action be performed is an overriding reason for performing the action in question – is prominent in the Old Testament. Any further thought about the matter is pointless; God's commands are to be obeyed without exception.

One powerful illustration of this idea is found in one of the most well-known episodes in the Old Testament. This is the binding of Isaac. Here are some of the highlights of the Biblical account:

> After these things God tested Abraham. He said to him, "Abraham!" And he said, "Here I am." He said, "Take your son, your only son Isaac, whom you love, and go to the land of Moriah, and offer him there as a burnt offering on one of the mountains that I shall show you." So Abraham rose early in the morning, saddled his donkey.... When they came to the place that God had shown him, Abraham built an altar there and laid the wood in order. He bound his son Isaac, and laid him on the altar, on top of the wood. Then Abraham reached out his hand and took the knife to kill his son. But the angel of the Lord called to him from heaven, and said, "Abraham, Abraham!" And he said, "Here I am." He said, "Do not lay your hand on the boy or do anything to him; for now I know that you fear God, since you have not withheld your son, your only son, from me."[10]

There is no indication in the Biblical account that Abraham questioned, hesitated, or had any doubts about whether he should sacrifice Isaac. Abraham did not ask God for any explanation of the command, nor did God provide one. The fact that God had commanded him to slaughter his only son, whom he loved, settled the matter; his only response, as far as we can see, was to get up early the next morning to carry out the order.

The two elements I have identified so far might not be so dangerous were they not combined with two other related elements. The first of these other two is the view that *there is a God who sometimes commands invasion, killing, and genocide – sometimes when there is no apparent justification for such actions other than that they have been commanded by God* (as in the binding of Isaac). The second related element is the view that *some people have the authority to order such activities on God's behalf*. These elements are dangerous because of the precedents they set. One alleged function of the Bible is to reveal the character of God: By learning the story of how God interacts with humanity through history, we learn something about the sort of being God is. And according to the Old Testament, one noteworthy feature of the Judeo-Christian God is that He is a God who sometimes orders His chosen people to wipe other groups of people from the face of the earth. Consider, for instance, the Old Testament account of God's promise to Moses of the conquest of Canaan:

> I am going to send an angel in front of you, to guard you on the way and to bring you to the place that I have prepared.... If you listen attentively to his voice and do all that I say, then I will be an enemy to your enemies and a foe to your foes. When my angel goes in front of you, and brings you to the Amorites, the Hittites, the Perizzites, the Canaanites, the Hivites, and the Jebusites, and I blot them out, you shall not bow down to their gods, or worship them, or follow their practices, but you shall utterly demolish them and break their pillars in pieces.... I will send my terror in front of you, and will throw into confusion all the people against whom you shall come, and I will make all your enemies turn their backs to you.[11]

If there is any doubt about what God means when He tells Moses that "you shall utterly demolish them," the Biblical account of the capture of the city of Jericho by the Israelites clears up the matter. I remember listening as a child to a song that recounted the victory of the Israelites at the battle of Jericho. The song related how the Israelites marched around the city of Jericho seven times, how they shouted and blew their trumpets, and how subsequently the walls of the city came tumbling down. Missing from the song, however, was the conclusion of the episode:

> So the people shouted, and the trumpets were blown. As soon as the people heard the sound of the trumpets, they raised a great shout, and the wall fell down flat; so the people charged straight ahead into the city and captured it. *Then they devoted to destruction by the edge of the*

sword all in the city, both men and women, young and old, oxen, sheep, and donkeys.[12]

For the idea that it is not just God but also His human representatives that can authorize such atrocities, consider the actions of Moses upon his return from Mount Sinai. Moses went up the mountain to receive the two stone tablets of God's covenant. In his absence, the Israelites constructed a golden calf, began worshipping it and, in general, began to run wild. Moses handled the situation as follows:

> When Moses saw that the people were running wild ... Moses stood in the gate of the camp, and said, "Who is on the Lord's side? Come to me!" And all the sons of Levi gathered around him. He said to them, "Thus says the Lord, the God of Israel, 'Put your sword on your side, each of you! Go back and forth from gate to gate throughout the camp, and each of you kill your brother, your friend, and your neighbor.'" The sons of Levi did as Moses commanded, and about three thousand of the people fell on that day. Moses said, "Today you have ordained yourselves for the service of the Lord, each one at the cost of a son or a brother, and so have brought a blessing on yourselves this day."[13]

Together, the four strands of thought I have identified form the view that *there is a God who has selected a particular group of people to be His chosen people, whose commands trump all other considerations, and who sometimes commands invasion, killing, and sacrifice – sometimes when there is no apparent justification for such actions other than that they have been commanded by God. Furthermore, human beings sometimes can have the authority to order such actions on God's behalf.*

Religious belief has had a wide variety of consequences. It can be a force for good: It can inspire people to perform admirable actions; it can offer them hope and enable them to endure the apparently unendurable; it can produce kindness, love, and compassion. For example, Karen Armstrong (1993) notes that the early Christian church was admired by pagans for "the welfare system that the churches had established and by the compassionate behavior of Christians toward one another."[14] But it must also be noted that with organized religion has come religious violence on a grand scale. It would be dishonest not to acknowledge that among the consequences of religious belief are rivers of tears, oceans of blood, and mountains of corpses.

Consider, for instance, Mark Juergensmeyer's (2000) brief account of the Christian Crusades:

> The nine Crusades – which began in 1095 with Pope Urban II's plea for Christians to rise up and re–take the Shrine of the Holy Sepulcher in Jerusalem, which had fallen into Muslim hands, and ended some three centuries later – were punctuated with the Christian battle cry *Deus volt* ("God wills it"). As the armies moved through Europe on their way to the Holy Land, they gathered the poor and desperate for quixotic adventures that led to virtually no military conquests of lasting value. They did, however, lead to the deaths of thousands of innocent Muslims and Jews.[15]

Armstrong connects the First Crusade with the books of the Bible in which the passages I have been discussing are found:

> During the long terrible march to Jerusalem, when the Crusaders narrowly escaped extinction, they could only account for their survival by assuming that they must be God's Chosen People, who enjoyed his special protection. He was leading them to the Holy Land as he had once lead the ancient Israelites. In practical terms, their God was still the primitive tribal deity of the early books of the Bible. When they finally conquered Jerusalem in the summer of 1099, they fell on the Jewish and Muslim inhabitants of the city with the zeal of Joshua and massacred them with a brutality that shocked even their contemporaries.[16]

The more widely the four ideas I have identified are accepted, the more we can expect such fanaticism and violence. The suggestion that these are ideas that we ought to inculcate in as many people as we can because doing so will be beneficial on the whole must be rejected. On the contrary, to introduce these ideas into a young mind is to poison it. Sincere and heartfelt acceptance of these beliefs turns a person into a killer-in-waiting; all that remains is to plug in the idea that he or she is among the chosen people (surely an enticing notion!) and that God or an authorized human representative has commanded him or her to kill. To such a mind, the idea is eminently plausible; after all, the believer has learned that this is precisely the sort of thing God sometimes commands. And God must be obeyed. Other religious ideas may at this point make a dangerous contribution. Perhaps the person is selfish; why should one's life be sacrificed on God's command? This sort of doubt is put to rest by the promise of eternal salvation in exchange for personal sacrifice. There is, after all, a divine guarantee of perfect justice. Perhaps the potential victim is, as far as can be seen innocent. But wasn't Isaac innocent as far as Abraham could see? And what is our understanding when compared with God's? We see but a tiny part of the whole; God sees the grand scheme. One's sense of the morality of the situation, independent of God's command, is not to be trusted. Juergensmeyer offers the following illustration:

> When the shy young man grinned into the videocamera the day before he was to become a martyr in a Hamas suicide operation, proclaiming that he was "doing this for Allah," he was demonstrating one of the remarkable facts about those who have committed acts of terrorism in the contemporary world: they would do virtually anything if they thought it had been sanctioned by divine mandate or conceived in the mind of God.[17]

Naturalism is devoid of these dangerous ideas. As there is no God, there is no group of people who have been singled out for special attention. Instead, we are all roughly in the same boat; the universe is equally indifferent and hostile toward each of us. The notion of a divinely chosen people tends to produce divisiveness; it perpetuates the sense that we in the chosen group are fundamentally different from the rest of humanity. Russell describes how naturalism, by contrast, can produce a sense of unity and comradeship between ourselves and the rest of humanity. The passage is somewhat lengthy but is worth quoting in its entirety:

> United with his fellow men by the strongest of all ties, the tie of a common doom, the free man finds that a new vision is with him always, shedding over every daily task the light of love. The life of man is a long march through the night, surrounded by invisible foes, tortured by weariness and pain, toward a goal that few can hope to reach, and where none may tarry long. One by one, as they march, our comrades vanish from our sight, seized by the silent orders of omnipotent death. Very brief is the time in which we can help them, in which their happiness or misery is decided. Be it ours to shed sunshine

on their path, to lighten their sorrows by the balm of sympathy, to give them the pure joy of a never–tiring affection, to strengthen failing courage, to instill faith in hours of despair. Let us not weigh in grudging scales their merits and demerits, but let us think only of their need – of the sorrows, the difficulties, perhaps the blindnesses, that make the misery of their lives; let us remember that they are fellow sufferers in the same darkness, actors in the same tragedy with ourselves. And so, when their day is over, when their good and their evil have become eternal by the immortality of the past, be it ours to feel that, where they suffered, no deed of ours was the cause; but wherever a spark of the divine fire kindled in their hearts, we were ready with encouragement, with sympathy, with brave words in which high courage glowed.[18]

The naturalist rejects the divisive cry of "no God but ours" (which always excludes more people than it includes) and replaces it with a cry of "there is no God to help us; we're all in this together," which applies to all human beings. In a naturalistic universe, there is no divine commander who is to be obeyed without question and whose commands settle, once and for all, what is to be done in a given situation. In a naturalistic universe, each of us must make the final determination about what is to be done in a given situation. Just as there is no infallible divine judge to whom we can pass off the difficult cases, there is also no infallible divine commander who can tell us what we should do. This is *not* to say that we can do whatever we want, or that we have the power to create our own meaning or our own morality however we see fit. The earlier chapters of this book were devoted to showing that meaning and morality exist independently of both the wills of human beings and of God (if He exists). Meaning and morality are discovered rather than created – but they must be discovered through the careful use of human reason rather than through divine revelation. In a naturalistic universe, this is the only option we have.

For all I have argued here, there may be supernatural beliefs whose widespread acceptance would be a good thing on the whole. But I think that any set of supernatural beliefs that includes the four dangerous Old Testament ideas I have identified here is not such a set. If Christianity falls into this category, then so much the worse for Christianity.

5.2 A CREED WE CAN LIVE BY?

The sort of view I have defended in this book sometimes goes by the name 'humanism.' In the concluding chapter of *Evil and Christian Ethics*, Gordon Graham argues that humanism is not a "creed we can live by." Graham writes:

> If humanism is true, the vast majority of human beings at all times, including the present, have had worthless lives. This is because their lives have contained little or nothing of those things which alone make them valuable from a humanistic point of view. This is the harsh side of humanism. . . . [19]

If there is an objection here, it is akin to the objection that students often raise to Aristotle's contention that the best possible human life is one spent in theoretical contemplation. Such an objection would run as follows:

1. If humanism is true, then most humans have lived lives devoid of internal meaning.
2. But it's not true that most humans have lived lives devoid of internal meaning.
3. Therefore, humanism is false.

There may be some room to quibble about the first premise, but I am willing to allow that something like it is true. In a naturalistic universe there is no afterlife, and so any internal meaning that a human life possesses is to be found in this earthly life. Yet many, perhaps even most humans throughout history, have lived in circumstances so dire as to preclude there being much or even any internal meaning in their lives.

The real weakness in the argument, of course, is in the second premise. What reason is there to accept it? All the empirical evidence we have tells against it; indeed, this very empirical evidence is part of the support for the first premise. Like my students' objection to Aristotle's view, Graham's objection seems to be based on the sense that *the universe just can't work that way.* But unless we have some reason to accept this idea, the argument simply begs the question. The idea that most human lives lack a significant degree of internal meaning is surely a depressing one, but being depressing and being false are two different things.

However, in the paragraph following the one I just quoted, Graham raises a more challenging objection:

> [T]he wealthy and privileged humanist has good grounds upon which to discount any talk of a moral obligation to seek reform of the world with a view to improving the lot of the poor and the ignorant. These grounds flow from a logical principle generally agreed, that 'ought implies can'; if the end result of our actions *cannot* be accomplished, we are under no obligation to attempt them.... The fortunate humanist's moral indifference is legitimated by practical impossibility. This is a result of the plain fact that there are very few circumstances, if any, in which he or she will have a realistic chance of increasing the humanistic value of the general run of people's lives.[20]

Recall the example of the people parachuting at random onto the widely varied surface of an alien planet. I suggested that people in such a situation would have an obligation to help their fellows. If naturalism is true, then we are in a relevantly similar situation, and so we have a similar obligation to help our fellow humans. Naturalistic humility consists in part in recognizing this aspect of our situation. This was the basis of my suggestion that naturalistic humility leads to charity.

But suppose that we add to the scenario the proviso that it is clear to everyone on the surface of the planet that nothing can be done to improve the general lot of everyone else. In this version of the scenario, no one would have an obligation to try to improve the general lot of everyone, since, as Graham points out, there can be no obligation to do what obviously cannot be done. Graham's suggestion is that in fact it is clear that there is nothing anyone can do to improve the general lot of humanity here on earth; hence, if naturalism is true, no one has any obligation to try.[21]

To respond to this argument, we must distinguish two claims:

1. There is nothing anyone can do to improve the lives of *all* (or most) humans.
2. There is nothing anyone can do to improve the lives of *some* humans.

To support his position, Graham discusses a variety of large-scale attempts to assist others, and argues that they have all failed. His argument is an inductive one: Given the past record of attempts to improve the human condition, the prospects that any future attempt might succeed are extremely dim. Graham does not deny that the general conditions of human life in at least some regions of the world have improved. What he denies is the claim that "the human condition has been bettered as a result of the self-conscious intention and design to better it."[22] He notes that "no serious historian subscribes any longer to the 'great men' conception which attributes large scale transformations to actions of individuals."[23] He also rejects the idea that states (rather than individuals) can bring about such large scale transformations:

> [W]e have only to consider the twentieth century's most conspicuous attempts to use the extended power of the state in the spirit of humanism to effect major transformations and improvements in the lot of ordinary people, to see how spectacularly they go wrong – the Bolshevik's socialist programme in Russia, the Nazi's attempts to create a Third Reich out of greater Germany, Mao's cultural revolution in China, Castro's policies in Cuba, the Khmer Rouge's brutal attempt to wipe the slate clean in Cambodia. . . . Schemes of humanistic political improvement, if the twentieth century is anything to go by, have an exceptionally bad record.[24]

Graham adds that when economic growth has occurred, "governments have *presided over* economic growth rather than *engineered* it," and he eventually reaches the following conclusion:[25]

> The intentional action of human beings individually or in concert at best accomplishes little and at worst is detrimental. . . . Humanism's implication is plain. The vast majority of human lives have lacked the values that make life worth living, a very great many lives will go on lacking them, and where this is the case there is nothing a convinced humanist can expect, or be expected, to do about it. . . . The creed of humanism is not . . . one of enlightened optimism, but either blind confidence or enlightened despair.[26]

Graham focuses exclusively on attempts by either individuals or states to effect massive, large-scale improvements. His position is that such attempts have failed in the past and hence we can expect all such future attempts to fail. Now, I think there is room for debate here; for example, was slavery not abolished in the United States? And wasn't this an intentionally brought about large-scale change that dramatically improved the lives of many slaves and their descendants?

Earlier I suggested that we pursue a program that might reasonably be construed as a program of the sort Graham criticizes.[27] I am referring to my suggestion that we put science to work in the service of the Platonic quest of finding a reliable way of making people virtuous. The track record of science, I submit, offers some hope in this endeavor. We have, after all, seen tremendous technological and scientific advance in the course of human history. And some of these advances have given at least some of us the ability to live lives that are far healthier and more comfortable than was previously possible. Of course scientific progress has hardly brought moral progress – but it is also true that science has not so far been used explicitly for that purpose. So I do not think that the kinds of failures Graham points to predict that the sort of program I have suggested is doomed to failure. In fact, I think a decent case could be made that in at least some of the examples Graham mentions, part of the problem was that the "schemes" in question were based on defective understandings of human nature, and this is exactly the sort of thing that progress in science, particularly in neuroscience, can help us avoid.[28] On the last page of his book *Looking for Spinoza*, Antonio Damasio writes: "No doubt the failure of past social engineering experiments is due, in some part, to the sheer folly of the plans or the corruption of their execution. But the failure also may have been due to the misconceptions of the human mind that informed the attempts."[29]

The main criticism I want to make of Graham's argument is that it at most establishes: (1) There is nothing anyone can do to improve the lives of most or all humans; but does little to establish (2) There is nothing anyone can do to improve the lives of some humans. Let us return to the parachute example once more. It may well be the case that there is nothing any individual can do to change radically the general conditions of the situation. The basic structure and

155

terrain of the planet, let us suppose, is unalterable, and no matter what anyone does, the trajectories taken by the parachutists will remain utterly random. It is consistent with all of this, however, that many individuals have the ability to help *some* of their fellows – and consequently these individuals have an obligation to do so. And I think that our situation is a lot like that.[30] Graham may be right that for most or all of us, massive transformation of the basic conditions of humanity is out of the question. But it is obvious that each of us (and by "us" I mean anyone living a life in which devoting significant time to reading a book like this is a reasonable option) is in a position to help someone.

In responding to the so-called "too high for humanity" objection to utilitarianism, John Stuart Mill writes:

> The multiplication of happiness is, according to the utilitarian ethics, the object of virtue: the occasions on which any person (except one in a thousand) has it in his power to do this on an extended scale – in other words, to be a public benefactor – are but exceptional; and on these occasions alone is he called on to consider public utility; in every other case, private utility, the interest or happiness of some few persons, is all he has to attend to.[31]

Recall as well Peter Singer's contemporary call for an ethical revolution. Singer writes that "[i]f 10 percent of the population were to take a consciously ethical outlook on life and act accordingly, the resulting change would be more significant than any change of government."[32] My response to Graham's argument, then, is the simple point that perhaps the best way to improve people's lives is not all at once but rather one person at a time. What is needed is not a savior, a "great man," or massive change imposed through political means, but rather something like Singer's ethical revolution.[33] Even in a naturalistic universe, each of us can help someone – and we are obligated to make the attempt.

There is another possible basis for the claim that naturalism is not a creed we can live by. This is the claim that naturalism is a world-view that is psychologically impossible for many people to accept throughout their entire lives. Recall Graham's repeated insistence that naturalism implies that most people are doomed to live

worthless or near-worthless lives. There is room to debate the per-
centages here, but naturalism surely implies that many people have
lived and will live such lives. If this is correct, then we can see why
it might be hard for many people to believe naturalism; is it possible
to live by a creed that implies that one is doomed to live a worthless
life? At the very least, a naturalistic universe allows for genuinely
hopeless situations. Christianity, by contrast, offers hope to anyone,
regardless of the situation. There is always the hope of eternal salvation. The transcendental temptation is hard to resist; if naturalism is
true, then many people may find that "[r]eality, looked at steadily,
is unbearable."[34]

My own sense is that naturalism is a creed that some can live by
and some cannot. What a person can believe varies depending on
external circumstances, constitutional makeup, and a host of other
factors. It seems clear that at least some people have been able to
live out their entire lives as naturalists. Russell apparently did so, as
did Freud.[35] David Hume also remained an atheist to the bitter end.
Indeed, Hume's die-hard atheism was a source of great consternation
to James Boswell, Samuel Johnson's biographer, who was a long-
time friend of Hume's and visited Hume while he lay dying. Boswell,
terrified by the thought of annihilation, was both fascinated and
repulsed by Hume's apparent calm acceptance of his own end.[36]

Empirical evidence that naturalism is not likely to gain wide acceptance appears in the book *Why God Won't Go Away*.[37] The book is
an examination of the neurological underpinnings of certain kinds
of religious experiences. Particular attention is paid to a type of mystical experience the authors dub "Absolute Unitary Being." This is
a state of mind in which there is "no sense of space or the passage
of time, no line between the self and the rest of the universe . . . no
subjective self at all . . . only . . . an absolute sense of unity".[38] The authors suggest that this type of mystical experience can arise from
the normal functioning of a healthy brain and that all normal human brains have the neurological equipment required to produce
Absolute Unitary Being. They suggest that this helps to explain why
religious belief will not go away: "This inherited ability to experience spiritual union is the real source of religion's staying power. It

anchors religious belief in something deeper and more potent than intellect and reason; it makes God a reality that can't be undone by ideas, and never grows obsolete."[39] The final chapter of the book ends with these words: "As long as our brains are arranged the way they are . . . spirituality will continue to shape the human experience, and God, however we define that majestic, mysterious concept, will not go away."[40]

It appears that we are, to some extent, hard-wired for religion. If this is correct, then presumably naturalists will always be in the minority. But of course it does not follow from this that naturalism is false. It may well be that naturalism is a fundamental truth about the universe that the majority of humans cannot accept, at least not for very long. It may be that many of us can accept it only while we are relatively young, healthy, and prosperous. If this is the case, then it may be that being able to face this fundamental fact about the universe is just one more benefit that accrues to those who are young, healthy, and prosperous.

How we should characterize the person who "finds religion" as a result of suffering, the loss of loved ones, the realization of impending death, or some other type of evil depends on whether naturalism or the relevant version of theism is true. C. S. Lewis would say that such a person has finally learned the lesson that God has been trying to teach him – that true happiness lies in God and not in earthly things.[41] Bertrand Russell would say that such a person has succumbed to fear and has been driven by desperation to adopt a superstition in order to avoid a truth he cannot face.

As I noted in the introduction, the goal of this book is not to determine whether naturalism is true or false, and so I will not attempt to settle the question of whether the person who finds religion has moved closer to or farther away from the truth. What I have tried to do in this book is to show that naturalism does not have some of the ethically repugnant implications that are often ascribed to it. Naturalism is not the same as, nor does it imply, nihilism, relativism, hedonism, or egoism. The naturalist can and should recognize that at least some human lives have internal meaning and that there are various moral obligations in virtue of an individual's position in the universe. If the central argument of *Why God Won't Go Away* (Newberg, D'Aquili, and Rause, 2001) is correct, then naturalism may never gain wide acceptance. But if naturalism is to be rejected, it should not be rejected on the basis of bad philosophy. Those who reject naturalism because they think it implies any of the ethical hobgoblins just listed do precisely that.

In his essay "Utility of Religion," Mill proposes that we adopt what he calls "the Religion of Humanity." This is a "religion" that is compatible with naturalism. Mill writes:

> The essence of religion is the strong and earnest direction of the emotions and desires towards an ideal object, recognized as of the highest excellence, and as rightfully paramount over all selfish objects of desire. This condition is fulfilled by the Religion of Humanity in as eminent a degree, and in as high a sense, as by the supernatural religions even in their best manifestations, and far more so than in any of their others.[42]

The "ideal object" of Mill's Religion of Humanity is, as the name suggests, humanity itself. At the heart of this "religion" is a "sense of unity with mankind, and a deep feeling for the general good."[43] What interests me here is not Mill's claim that the view he describes is a religion but rather his suggestion that one of the main benefits of religion is *the defeat of selfishness*. Pascal says of Christianity that "[n]o other religion has held that we should hate ourselves."[44] As we have seen, both Pascal and C. S. Lewis emphasize that genuine happiness and virtue are to be obtained through submission to God. Lewis writes: "[T]he proper good of a creature is to surrender itself to its Creator – to enact intellectually, volitionally, and emotionally, that relationship which is given in the mere fact of its being a creature. When it does so, it is good and happy."[45]

The main obstacle to this surrender is selfishness, which Lewis and Pascal understand as love of the self, or more precisely, as loving the self more than God. When Pascal says that Christianity teaches hatred of the self, what he is getting at is the idea that Christianity teaches surrender to God, the primary obstacle to which is excessive self-love.[46]

But one does not have to be a theist, much less a Christian, to recognize that the tendency toward selfishness is at the same time one of the most entrenched as well as the most pernicious features of human nature. Naturalist and theist alike should acknowledge that one of the greatest challenges we face is the dark heart within ourselves. To combat this heart of darkness, Christianity recommends surrender to God; Mill recommends developing a sense of unity with mankind; Kant recommends making the requirements of morality our top priority; Singer recommends devoting oneself to the reduction of suffering; I have recommended putting science to use in the Platonic quest for a reliable way of making people virtuous. These are all forms of a common struggle – the struggle against the selfishness inherent in human nature. Perhaps, then, this is one struggle in which we are all on the same side. Long live the ethical revolution.

NOTES

Introduction

1. M. Night Shyamalan, dir. *Signs*, Film. Touchstone Pictures, (2002). Armand Nicholi, Jr., makes much the same point in *The Question of God* (New York: Free Press, 2002), 7: "Most of us make one of two basic assumptions: we view the universe as a result of random events and life on this planet as a matter of chance; or we assume an Intelligence beyond our universe who gives the universe order, and life meaning."

2. Alvin Plantinga, *Warranted Christian Belief* (Oxford: Oxford Univ. Press, 2000), 228. For a more complete but still accessible version of the story, see Ernst Mayr, *What Evolution Is* (New York: Basic Books, 2001).

3. This brief psychological account contains, of course, no *arguments* against Christianity.

4. Arguments distinct from the two kinds I will discuss have been proposed. It might be suggested, for instance, that religious experience can make it irrational for one to fail to accept Christianity. I have, so far, had no such experiences.

5. The argument has a long history, going back at least as far as the Platonic dialogue *Timaeus*. Some important contemporary discussions are: Richard Dawkins, *The Blind Watchmaker* (New York: W.W. Norton & Company, 1996); Michael Behe, *Darwin's Black Box* (New York: Touchstone, 1996); Robert Pennock, *Tower of Babel* (Cambridge, MA: MIT Press, 1999); and Del Ratzsch, *Nature, Design, and Science* (New York: SUNY Press, 2001). The literature on this topic is continuously expanding.

6. For a useful discussion, see Peter van Inwagen, *Metaphysics* (Boulder, CO: Westview Press, 1993), 132–48.

7. David Hume, *Dialogues Concerning Natural Religion*, 2nd ed. (Indianapolis: Hackett, 1998), 75. For a contemporary revival of Philo's position, see Paul Draper, "Pain and Pleasure: An Evidential Problem for Theists," *NOUS* 23 (1989), 331–50.

8. Hume, "Of Miracles," in *Dialogues*, 112.

9. Ibid., 122.
10. Corey Washington illustrated Hume's position with a nice series of examples during his February 9, 1995, debate with William Lane Craig at the University of Washington. The examples are given toward the end of Washington's second rebuttal; a transcript is available online, www.infidels.org/library/modern/corey_washington/craig-washington/washington3.html (accessed March 26, 2004).
11. C. S. Lewis, *Miracles* (New York: HarperCollins, 2001), 2 (my emphasis). Lewis goes on to argue for the probability of miracles.
12. Karen Armstrong, *A History of God* (New York: Ballantine Books, 1993), 79. Intellectual honesty requires that I acknowledge that in Lee Strobel's *The Case for Christ* (Grand Rapids, MI: Zondervan, 1998), 34, Craig Blomberg claims that the gospel of Mark was written "no later than about 60 A.D., maybe even the late 50s."
13. Strobel, *Case for Christ*, 222 (my emphasis). This is the most important page in Strobel's book.
14. Hume, "Miracles," 123.
15. [www.brainyquote-com/quotes/authors/s/stephen_roberts.html] Accessed September 12, 2004.
16. Plutarch, *The Rise and Fall of Athens: Nine Greek Lives*, trans. I. Scott-Kilvert (New York: Penguin Books, 1960), 92.
17. For a critical discussion of historical arguments for the truth of certain central Christian claims about Jesus by a contemporary Christian philosopher, see Plantinga, *Christian Belief*, 268–80.

1. God and the Meaning of Life

1. Plato, *Euthyphro, Apology, Crito*, trans. F. J. Church (New York: Macmillian, 1948), 37.
2. According to the Shorter Scottish Catechism, at any rate.
3. See, for instance, Alvin Plantinga, *Christian Belief*, 489.
4. William Lane Craig, "The Absurdity of Life Without God," hisdefense.org/audio/wc_audio.html (accessed March 26, 2004). Some of the ideas contained in Craig's talk are also present in a speech given by the character Meursault toward the end of Albert Camus's novel *The Stranger*, trans. Stuart Gilbert (New York: Random House, 1946), 152.
5. For an interesting critical discussion of the view that a life is meaningful to the extent that the one who lives it fulfills some divinely assigned purpose, see Thaddeus Metz, "Could God's Purpose Be the Source of Life's Meaning?" *Religious Studies* 36 (2000), 293–313.
6. Susan Wolf, "The Meanings of Lives," www.law.nyu.edu/clppt/program 2003/readings/wolf.pdf (accessed March 26, 2004), 21.
7. The example also suggests that supernatural meaning is not sufficient for internal meaning. Sisyphus has been given a mission by the gods, but it is a mission designed to strip his life of any value for him.

8. Richard Taylor, *Good and Evil* (Amherst, NY: Prometheus Books, 2000), 333–4.

9. In *Atheism, Morality, and Meaning* (Amherst, NY: Prometheus Books, 2002), 201, Michael Martin suggests that Taylor's proposal here is that "[a] life is meaningful if and only if it is lived in the way it is natural to live it." I think my own formulation is preferable because it is clearer and seems to fit better with Taylor's discussion of the case of Sisyphus. Taylor's idea is that the gods could give Sisyphus' life meaning by instilling in him the *desire* to roll stones.

10. Taylor, *Good and Evil*, 332.

11. Leo Tolstoy, "My Confession," in *The Meaning of Life*, 2nd ed., ed. E. D. Klemke (Oxford: Oxford Univ. Press, 2000), 12.

12. Ibid., 12.

13. Ibid., 13–14.

14. Taylor, *Good and Evil.*, 333.

15. Plato, *Apology*, 45.

16. Stephen Darwall, "Valuing Activity," in *Human Flourishing*, eds. E. F. Paul, F. D. Miller, Jr., and J. Paul (Cambridge: Cambridge Univ. Press, 1999), 176.

17. Michael Martin reaches a similar conclusion, noting that Taylor's proposal "errs on the side of lenience" because it "allows practically any life . . . to be meaningful." See Martin, *Atheism*, 205–6. For a related discussion with a similar conclusion, see John Cottingham, *On the Meaning of Life* (New York: Routledge, 2003), 16–18.

18. Taylor, *Good and Evil*, 323.

19. I use the term "intrinsic value" to express what Thomas Hurka calls the "strict definition" of intrinsic value; see Thomas Hurka, "Two Kinds of Organic Unity," *The Journal of Ethics* 2:4 (1998), 301. Some contemporary philosophers have suggested that the term "intrinsic value" can be used to refer to kinds of value that do not depend exclusively on a thing's intrinsic properties. Hurka is open to this suggestion and Shelly Kagan offers an extended argument for it in his "Rethinking Intrinsic Value," *Journal of Ethics* 2:4 (1998), 277–97. For present purposes, I will simply stipulate that "intrinsic value" means intrinsic value in the strict sense; this is the kind of intrinsic value that is most relevant to the central project of this book.

20. G. E. Moore, *Principia Ethica* (Cambridge: Cambridge Univ. Press, 1903), 91.

21. For a useful discussion of various varieties of extrinsic value, see Ben Bradley, "Extrinsic Value," *Philosophical Studies* 91 (1998), 109–26.

22. Peter Singer, *How Are We to Live? Ethics in an Age of Self-Interest* (Amherst, NY: Prometheus Books, 1995), 195.

23. Ibid., 213 (my emphasis).

24. Ibid., 216 (my emphasis).

25. Ibid., 195. For example, in discussing the case of Sisyphus, Singer suggests that Sisyphus could bring meaning into his life by actually *building* a beautiful and enduring temple.
26. A similar (though not identical) conclusion is reached by Wolf (see "Meanings," 6–12). Like Taylor, Wolf approaches the issue of meaningfulness by first considering meaninglessness; instead of Sisyphus, she considers (among others) the case of "The Blob," who "spends day after day, or night after night, in front of a television set, drinking beer and watching situation comedies."
27. Singer, *How?*, 218.
28. A similar proposal is made by Kai Nielsen, who remarks that "A man who says, 'If God is dead, nothing matters,' is a spoilt child who has never looked at his fellowman with compassion" (*Ethics Wihout God*, rev. ed. (New York: Prometheus Books, 1990), 117–18).
29. Aristotle, *Nicomachean Ethics*, trans. Martin Ostwald (Englewood Cliffs, NJ: Prentice Hall, 1962), 8, NE 1095b15–20.
30. Ibid., NE 10.6–8.
31. Darwall, "Valuing Activity," 176 (my emphasis).
32. Rene Descartes, *Discourse on Method and Meditations*, trans. L. J. Lafleur (New York: Macmillan, 1960), 92.
33. Plato, *Philebus*, trans. D. Frede (Indianapolis: Hackett, 1993), 16, 21d.
34. Aristotle, *Ethics.*, 8, NE 1095b20.
35. Ibid., 288, NE 1177a5–10.
36. The Roman philosopher Boethius concurred (see *The Consolation of Philosophy*, trans. V. E. Watts (New York: Penguin, 1969), 90).
37. Robert Nozick, *Anarchy, State, and Utopia* (New York: Basic Books, 1977), 44.
38. Epicurus, *Letters, Principal Doctrines, and Vatican Sayings* (New York: Macmillan, 1964), 57, 131b.
39. John Stuart Mill, *Utilitarianism* (Indianapolis: Hackett, 1979), 8.
40. Kohn, Alfie. (1986). *No Contest: The case against competition*. (Boston: Houghtin Mifflin), 111.
41. Marquis de Sade, *The Misfortunes of Virtue and Other Early Tales*, trans. D. Coward (Oxford: Oxford Univ. Press, 1992), 99–100.
42. Singer, *How?*, 220.
43. Ibid., 235.
44. Ibid., 222.
45. Ibid., 231.
46. Paul Edwards, "The Meaning and Value of Life," in *Meaning of Life*, ed. E.D. Klemke, 140.
47. Marcus Aurelius, *Meditations*, trans. J. Collier (London: Walter Scott Publishing Co. Ltd., 1805), 52.
48. Thomas Nagel, *Mortal Questions* (Cambridge: Cambridge Univ. Press, 1979), 11.
49. Aristotle, *Ethics*, 3, NE 1094a1–5.

50. This interpretation is somewhat controversial, but for a compelling defense of it see Richard Kraut, *Aristotle on the Human Good* (Princeton, NJ. Princeton Univ. Press, 1989).
51. Aristotle, *Ethics*, 292–3, NE 1178b10–25.
52. Plato, *Republic*, trans. G. M. A. Grube (Indianapolis: Hackett, 1992), 148, 473d.
53. John Milton, *Paradise Lost* (Chicago: The Great Books Foundation, 1956), 187, Book VIII, lines 160–80.
54. Ibid., 222, Book IX, lines 708–9; also see Genesis 3:4–5.
55. Taylor, *Good and Evil*, 331.
56. An activity can be *both* intrinsically and extrinsically good. I should note that my main goal here is not to provide a complete answer to the question "what is the meaning of life?" but instead to make plausible the claim that life can have meaning even if God does not exist. For more systematic secular accounts of the meaning of life, see Paul Kurtz, "The Meaning of Life," in *In Defense of Secular Humanism* (Amherst, NY: Prometheus Books, 1983a), 153–68; and Owen Flanagan, *The Problem of the Soul* (New York: Basic Books, 2002), 279–86.
57. Craig, "Absurdity of Life."
58. Tolstoy, "My Confession," 14.
59. See also Wolf, "Meanings," 23.
60. Spike Jonze, dir. *Adaptation*. Film. (Columbia Pictures, 2002).

2. God and Morality

1. Plato, *Euthyphro*, 6e–7a, trans. Scott Senn.
2. The sort of possibility involved here is the familiar (yet somewhat mysterious) "broadly logical possibility" appealed to by Alvin Plantinga and other contemporary philosophers of religion. (See Alvin Plantinga, *The Nature of Necessity* (Oxford: Oxford Univ. Press, 1974), 1–9). Appealing to the concept of a possible world, we can say that X exists contingently just in case (1) X exists in the actual world and (2) there is some (metaphysically) possible world in which X does not exist.
3. X exists necessarily just in case X exists in every possible world.
4. Philip Quinn, "The Primacy of God's Will in Christian Ethics," in *Christian Theism and Moral Philosophy* (Macon, GA: Mercer Univ. Press, 1998), 263.
5. The view captured by these two theses is different from the view Quinn later proposes; specifically, Quinn does not endorse the Control Thesis, 263–4.
6. Logical consistency is weaker than broad metaphysical possibility; roughly, a proposition P is logically consistent just in case a contradiction cannot be derived from it via the standard laws of logic. Still, the Control Thesis does not ascribe to God the power to make *any* ethical claim true. For instance, that a given action is morally right and that it is not the case that that action is morally right is both an ethical claim

and logically inconsistent; the Control Thesis is not to be understood as ascribing to God the power to make such a claim true.

7. William Lane Craig, "The Absurdity of Life Without God." Craig often argues from the existence of "objective moral values" to the existence of God. For transcripts of some of Craig's debates, see www.leaderu.com/offices/billcraig/menus/debates.html (accessed March 26, 2004).

8. One who holds the Dependency Thesis merely as a contingent truth can consistently maintain that while God is in fact the author of all ethical truth, there are possible worlds with ethical truths in which God does not exist. In such worlds the ethical truths have some source other than God.

9. Craig, "Absurdity of Life."

10. Hume, *Dialogues*, 63.

11. John Mackie, "Evil and Omnipotence," in *The Problem of Evil: Selected Readings*, ed. M. L. Peterson (Notre Dame: Univ. of Notre Dame Press, 1992), 97.

12. Ibid., 98.

13. Plantinga's version of the free will defense may be found in a variety of sources; I will refer to "The Free Will Defense," Chapter 2 of *The Analytic Theist: An Alvin Plantinga Reader*, ed. J. F. Sennett (Grand Rapids: Wm. B. Eerdmans, 1998), 22–49.

14. Ibid., 37.

15. Ibid., 43–4; I have ignored some technical subtleties here, but nothing in what follows turns on them.

16. Assume that the situations include the fact that the beings in them are free to choose either possible alternative. The last two statements ignore the technical subtlety that, strictly speaking, the situation Bill faces when Ted is present is distinct from the situation Bill faces when Ted is not present – but again, nothing in my argument turns on this.

17. Plantinga bases his free will defense on the possibility that every individual essence suffers from *transworld depravity*. Those interested in technical subtleties will be interested to observe that my model shows that Plantinga could actually get by with a weaker claim. If an essence suffers from transworld depravity, this implies that any world that God could actualize in which that essence is instantiated and is free is one in which *that very individual* does something wrong. But Plantinga could get by with the weaker claim that it is possible that every individual essence is such that any world that God could actualize in which that essence is instantiated and is free is one in which *somebody – but not necessarily the individual in question* – does something wrong. For instance, in the simple model at hand, Ted does not suffer from transworld depravity; nevertheless, God cannot actualize a world containing free creatures in which no one does something wrong.

18. I recently faced a similar situation when confronted with the task of producing a seating arrangement for my wedding.

19. Plantinga, "Free Will Defense," 27.
20. John Hick, *Evil and the God of Love* (New York: Macmillan, 1966), 290.
21. Ibid., 293.
22. Ibid., 291.
23. According to Hick, God in fact cannot bring about the great good in question without introducing evil into the world because the great good *entails* the presence of evil in the world. So Hick's proposal follows the version of the schema in the parentheses. On Plantinga's view, it may be that God cannot bring about the great good in question without introducing evil into the world – not because the great good entails evil but rather for the more complicated reason described above. Plantinga's proposal follows the version of the schema outside of the parentheses.
24. Ralph Cudworth, *A Treatise Concerning Eternal and Immutable Morality* (New York: Garland, 1976), 9–10.
25. Edward Wierenga, "A Defensible Divine Command Theory," *Nous* 17 (September 1983), 394.
26. Some might find this counterfactual, with its impossible antecedent, puzzling; the intelligibility of such counterfactuals is defended by Linda Zagzebski in "What If the Impossible Had Been Actual?" in *Christian Theism and the Problems of Philosophy*, ed. M. Beatty (Notre Dame: Univ. of Notre Dame Press, 1990), 165–83.
27. For an illuminating discussion of the distinction between having the power to do something and being capable of doing that very thing, see Thomas Morris, *Our Idea of God* (Notre Dame: Univ. of Notre Dame Press, 2000), 66–73.
28. As I noted when I first introduced the concept of intrinsic value, I am working with what Hurka calls the "strict definition" of intrinsic value; see Section 1.4.
29. The same kind of objection would apply to the suggestion explored by Quinn that ethical truths are dependent on God's *beliefs* (see Quinn, "Primacy of God's Will," 268.) Perhaps Quinn would claim only that human obligations are dependent on God's beliefs. I will discuss this approach later in this chapter.
30. Roderick Chisholm, *The Problem of the Criterion* (Milwaukee, WI: Marquette Univ. Press, 1973), 21.
31. Kai Nielsen, *Ethics Without God*, 10.
32. This argument bears on Robert Adams's suggestion that "all and only those things that resemble God are excellent" (Robert Adams, *Finite and Infinite Goods* (Oxford: Oxford Univ. Press, 1999). 29). What Adams calls 'excellence' can only be a kind of extrinsic value because whether a thing has it or not depends on the extent to which it *resembles* God – and this is a relational rather than intrinsic property. The argument I have sketched shows that excellence is not the only kind of goodness in the universe.

33. As before, the type of necessity involved here is broadly logical necessity or metaphysical necessity rather than strict logical necessity.

34. The ideas developed in the three previous paragraphs are similar to some suggestions made by Richard Swinburne in "Duty and the Will of God," in *Divine Commands and Morality*, ed. P. Helm (Oxford: Oxford Univ. Press, 1981), 125–6.

35. Unless of course your friend is an alcoholic whose driver's license was revoked for driving under the influence; or he is narcoleptic; or. . . . But let us suppose none of the infinitely many circumstances of this sort that may be true are not.

36. At least, given the state of technology as I write this in May of 2003.

37. On the other hand, if God does not exist, we may have moral obligations that we would not have if God did exist.

38. Wierenga calls it this in "Divine Command," 389.

39. Plato, *Phaedo*, trans. G. M. A. Grube (Indianapolis: Hackett, 1977), 10, 62b.

40. See, for example, Exodus 19:5 and Deuteronomy 7:6.

41. Baruch Brody, "Morality and Religion Reconsidered," in *Readings in the Philosophy of Religion*, ed. B. Brody (Englewood Cliffs, NJ: Prentice Hall, 1974), 601.

42. I assume that Brody intends the "possible claim" to be necessarily true if true at all. The assumption is reasonable for our purposes whether it is Brody's intent or not, since the claim implies Karamazov's Thesis only if it is necessarily true. If the claim is merely contingently true, this leaves open the possibility that while in the actual world all our moral obligations derive from the fact that we belong to God, the nearest possible world in which God does not exist is one in which we have moral obligations deriving from some other source.

43. Brody, "Morality and Religion," 601.

44. Ibid.

45. Ibid., 595.

46. Adams, *Finite and Infinite*, 252.

47. Richard Mouw, *The God Who Commands* (Notre Dame: Univ. of Notre Dame Press, 1996), 19–20.

48. Adams, *Finite and Infinite*, 253–4.

49. Ibid., 255.

50. Hick, *God of Love*, 132–3.

51. For an account of a somewhat more complicated ground, see Chapter 3 of John Hare's *God's Call* (Grand Rapids MI: Wm. B. Eerdmans, 2001), particularly 110–11.

52. We can already see this in an uninteresting way: The considerations just mentioned, if correct, seem to imply the truth of certain ethical principles – principles such as, for instance, we ought to obey the commands of a being who has given us every good thing that we have. Some of

these principles could be true even if God does not exist, in which case we might vacuously live up to them. So in a sense we would have certain obligations even if God did not exist. But if these were the only obligations we had, this would be a pretty uninteresting sense since there would be no action a person could perform that would constitute a violation of a moral obligation.

53. Mark Murphy, "Divine Command, Divine Will, and Moral Obligation," *Faith and Philosophy* 15:1 (January 1998), 4; I have revised Murphy's formulations slightly.
54. Ibid., 16.
55. Ibid., 20.
56. Ibid., 20.
57. Adams, *Finite and Infinite*, 260.
58. Ibid., 261.
59. Milton, *Paradise Lost*, 192, Book VIII, lines 369–72.
60. Ibid., 193–4, Book VIII, lines 399–411.
61. Ibid., 194–5, Book VIII, lines 437–48.
62. Adams, *Finite and Infinite*, 261.
63. Ibid., 265.
64. Mouw, *God who Commands*, 19–20
65. This claim must be qualified somewhat. God might be able to impose some such obligations in roundabout fashion. Suppose, for example, that God wants to bring it about that you are obligated to perform action A. God could bring it about that a suitably qualified human being – one you recognize as being authorized to impose certain obligations on you – commands you to perform action A. But God could not impose obligations on reasonable naturalists in the relatively direct fashion envisaged by Adams.
66. Adams, *Finite and Infinite*, 270.
67. The unreasonable naturalist may even be open to moral criticism. Suppose, for example, that formerly the naturalist was a theist but intentionally became a naturalist to avoid God's imposed obligations. Such an action may well be open to moral criticism on the theistic view.
68. Moore, *Principia Ethica*, 147.
69. William Lane Craig, "The Indispensability of Theological Metaethical Foundations for Morality," 1996, home.apu.edu/~CTRF/papers/1996_papers/craig.html (accessed March 26, 2004).
70. For one such attempt, see Martin, *Atheism, Morality, and Meaning*, Chapters 3 and 4.
71. Plato, *Apology*, 4.
72. Ibid., 11.
73. For some fascinating research concerning the views of children from a variety of religious traditions on some of the issues raised in this chapter, see Chapter 2 of Larry Nucci, *Education in the Moral Domain* (Cambridge:

Cambridge Univ. Press, 2001), 33. On the basis of his research, Nucci claims that "even for deeply religious children from fundamentalist or orthodox backgrounds, morality stems from criteria independent of God's word."
74. Exodus 20:4–5.
75. John Leslie, *Universes* (New York: Routledge, 1989), 165–6. Leslie himself favors a view he labels "Neoplatonism," according to which God *is* the ethical requirements themselves.
76. Obviously "passing judgment" is to be understood metaphorically here; more precisely, these truths imply certain other truths about the actions and character of God (if one exists) and humans.

3. The Divine Guarantee of Perfect Justice

1. Plato, *Republic*, 36, 360c.
2. William Lane Craig, "Indispensability."
3. Simon Blackburn, *Ruling Passions* (Oxford: Oxford Univ. Press, 1998), 265. The same distinction is sometimes drawn in terms of subjective vs. objective reasons.
4. The account of why I am not a Christian in my introduction had two parts. The first part presented some psychological reasons why I never accepted Christianity; the second presented some normative reasons why I persist in rejecting it.
5. Except insofar as doing our duty is accidentally connected with our own self-interest; but Craig thinks that no such connection exists in many cases, and in cases of that sort, we have no reason to do our duty if naturalism is true.
6. Hereafter I shall drop the term 'normative' and just speak of reasons. In doing so I intend to speak of normative reasons. Primarily for the sake of simplicity and clarity, I have presented a very strong version of the challenge here; the conclusion is surely too strong because in at least some cases self-interest and morality coincide. Stating the challenge in this stark way, though, will help us to understand better the various strategies for responding to it.
7. In *Republic, Nicomachean Ethics,* and *An Enquiry Concerning the Principles of Morals* (Oxford: Oxford Univ. Press, 1998) respectively. Singer's position in the final two chapters of *How Are We To Live?* (discussed in Chapter 1) is a contemporary example of this type of approach. Freud also apparently pursued this kind of strategy; see Armand Nicholi, Jr., *The Question of God* (New York: Free Press, 2002), 72.
8. Craig, "Indispensability."
9. As before, this interpretation is controversial; for a defense, see Richard Kraut, *Aristotle on Good.*
10. Aristotle, *Nicomachean Ethics*, 262–3, NE1169a20–30.

11. Ibid.
12. For a more extensive discussion and defense of this interpretation of Aristotle's view, see my "Egoism and *Eudaimonia*-Maximization in the *Nicomachean Ethics*," *Oxford Studies in Ancient Philosophy*, Volume XXVI (2004), 277–95.
13. The basis for this claim is the much–discussed function (*ergon*) argument of NE 1.7 of Aristotle's *Ethics*. I will not undertake a discussion of that argument here, but it is worth noting that, even if this argument fails, it does not follow that Aristotle's axiology is false.
14. David Hume, *Enquiry*, 153.
15. Ibid., 155.
16. Ibid.
17. Mill, *Utilitarianism*, 13.
18. Of course, whether these kinds of concerns produce pleasure or pain depends on how the team is doing.
19. Mill, *Utilitarianism*, 13.
20. See Aristotle, *Ethics*, 26, NE 1100b35.
21. Hume, *Enquiry*, 156.
22. Robert Frank, *Passions Within Reason* (New York: W.W. Norton, 1988), 78.
23. For a more recent and detailed discussion of this phenomenon, as well as some critical discussion of Frank's book, see Jon Elster, *Ulysses Unbound* (Cambridge: Cambridge Univ. Press, 2000), Chapter 1.
24. Frank, *Passions*, 82.
25. Ibid., 18. Frank also argues that human beings are pretty good at directly discerning the character traits of others in relatively brief periods of time. In short, we have a pretty good knack for telling the difference between sensible knaves and the genuinely virtuous; see Chapters 2, 3, 5, 6, and 7 of Frank's book. This claim, if correct, constitutes another reason why genuine virtue is a more promising route to happiness than is sensible knavery (opportunism). But also see John Doris, *Lack of Character* (Cambridge: Cambridge Univ. Press, 2002), particularly Chapter 5, for considerations that suggest that Frank's position may need significant qualification; perhaps what Frank's data really reveal is that people are pretty good at detecting relatively specific, local dispositions – for instance, the disposition to cooperate (or defect) when playing "prisoner's dilemma." Doris argues that commonsense views about moral character are at odds with the dramatic influence of situational factors on our behavior. His central thesis is that the available empirical evidence suggests that human beings are entirely (or almost entirely) devoid of character traits as they are traditionally understood; a full treatment of Doris's book is beyond the scope of the present work, but his arguments are fascinating and worthy of serious attention. For one useful critical discussion, see Christian Miller, "Social Psychology and Virtue Ethics," *Journal of Ethics* 7 (2003), 365–92.

26. Immanuel Kant, *The Metaphysics of Morals*, trans. M. Gregor (Cambridge: Cambridge Univ. Press, 1996), 155.
27. Immanuel Kant, *Groundwork of the Metaphysic of Morals*, trans. H. J. Paton (New York: Torchbook, 1964), 82.
28. Immanuel Kant, *Religion Within the Limits of Reason Alone*, trans. T. M. Greene and H. H. Hudson (New York: Harper & Row, 1960), 31–2.
29. It turns out, therefore, that Kant's "evil man" corresponds closely to Hume's sensible knave and Frank's opportunist.
30. Immanuel Kant, *Lectures on Ethics*, trans. L. Infield (Indianapolis, Hackett: 1930), 76.
31. Immanuel Kant, *Critique of Practical Reason*, trans. M. Gregor (Cambridge: Cambridge Univ. Press, 1997), 104. John Hare discusses Kant's argument in Chapter 3 of *The Moral Gap* (Oxford: Clarendon Press, 1996), 69–96. There, Hare distinguishes between a highest good in a more ambitious sense and a highest good in a less ambitious sense. My specification of Kant's highest good corresponds to Hare's highest good in the more ambitious sense. Hare claims that the starting point of Kant's moral argument in the *Critique* is the claim that the highest good in the more ambitious sense is possible. I agree. Hare's highest good in the less ambitious sense corresponds to just the second component of the Kantian highest good.
32. Kant, *Critique*, 104.
33. Ibid., 105.
34. Ibid.
35. In doing this, I do not mean to suggest that the considerations I will explore are any part of Kant's argument in the relevant section of the *Critique* – though some of the considerations are pointed to by Kant elsewhere.
36. Genesis 8:21.
37. C. S. Lewis, *The Problem of Pain* (New York: HarperCollins, 2001), 63.
38. Kant, *Critique*, 102.
39. Kant, *Lectures*, 246.
40. Matthew 7:1.
41. C. S. Lewis, *Mere Christianity* (New York: HarperCollins, 2001), 91.
42. Kant, *Lectures*, 80. For a quite different kind of argument for the conclusion that we ought not try to judge the character of others, see Doris, *Lack of Character*.
43. Kant, *Metaphysics*, 196.
44. Ibid., 155. Similar remarks may be found in Kant's *Religion Within Limits*, 33.
45. Joseph Conrad, *The Heart of Darkness* (New York: Penguin Books, 1976), 44.
46. Ibid., 92.
47. Ibid., 107–8.
48. Kant, *Metaphysics*, 155.

49. Conrad, *Darkness*, 124–5.
50. Ibid., 130–1. In *Lack of Character*, Doris argues that research in social psychology suggests that we are all a lot more like Kurtz than we might think; we may all be, to a certain significant extent, "hollow at the core." See Chapter 3 of Doris's book, particularly the discussion of Milgram's obedience experiments and the Stanford prison experiment. These two experiments seem to have generated less extreme, real-life experiences of the sort Kurtz went through.
51. Lewis, *Pain*, 94.
52. Blaise Pascal, *Pensees and Other Writings*, trans. Honor Levi (Oxford: Oxford Univ. Press, 1995), #182, 54. Also see Boethius, *Consolation of Philosophy*, 99–104.
53. Lewis, *Pain*, 94–5. Elsewhere Lewis suggests that "the real problem is not why some humble, pious, believing people suffer, but why some do *not*" (104). Actually this is a serious problem for Lewis's view; ironically, his solution to the problem of pain may fall prey to a problem of a *lack* of pain. But I will not explore this point here.
54. Ibid., 114–16.
55. John Hick's "vale of soul–making" theodicy (*Evil and God of Love*) discussed in Chapter 2 here, also seems to have this implication. According to that view, God imposes undeserved suffering on some in order to afford them the opportunity to improve their moral characters through their own free choices.
56. There is some psychological evidence that we can make mistakes about the nature of our own motivation as well and, in some cases, agents are actually *worse* at recognizing the causes of their own behavior than are outside observers. See, for instance, Richard Nisbett and Timothy Wilson, "Telling More than We Can Know: Verbal Reports on Mental Processes," *Psychological Review* 84 (1977), 231–59, and Richard Nisbett and Lee Ross, *Human Inference: Strategies and Shortcomings of Social Judgment* (Englewood Cliffs, NJ: Prentice Hall, 1980), particularly 195–227.
57. John Cottingham, *On the Meaning of Life* (New York: Routledge, 2003), 76–7.
58. Kant, *Critique*, 104 (my emphasis).
59. Thanks to an anonymous reader for helping me to clarify this point.
60. Craig, "Indispensability." The report is from Richard Wurmbrand, *Tortured for Christ* (London: Hodder & Stoughton, 1967), 34.
61. Jonathan Sumption, *The Albigensian Crusade* (London: Faber and Faber, 1978), 48.
62. Ibid., 93.
63. Other cases are not difficult to find; Exodus 32:25–9 and Joshua 6:15–21 describe two particularly horrendous examples.
64. I do not mean to suggest that Christians are committed to the view that the conquerors acted properly; I claim only that Christians are committed to the view that the conquerors were right in thinking that

God would punish or reward each of their victims appropriately. Craig does suggest that the atheist is committed to the view that there is nothing wrong with the way the Communist torturers behaved. Indeed, as we have seen, Craig maintains that the atheist is committed to the view that there is nothing wrong with the way anyone behaves. I think we have also seen that Craig is wrong about this.

65. Steven Pinker, *The Blank Slate: The Modern Denial of Human Nature* (New York: Penguin Putnam, 2002), 189.
66. This is the so-called "deprivation view" about the badness of death; for a defense of this view, see Fred Feldman, *Confrontations with the Reaper* (Oxford: Oxford Univ. Press, 1992).
67. George Mavrodes, "Religion and the Queerness of Morality," in *Moral Philosophy: A Reader*, ed. L. Pojman (Indianapolis: Hackett, 1993), 257.
68. Bertrand Russell, "Why I Am Not a Christian," in *Why I Am Not a Christian and Other Essays on Religion and Related Subjects*, ed. P. Edwards (New York: Simon & Schuster, 1957), 13.
69. Gordon Graham, *Evil and Christian Ethics* (Cambridge: Cambridge Univ. Press, 2001), 77.
70. Ibid., 88.
71. Ibid. Presumably it is the enslaving of one human by another that Graham has in mind.
72. Ibid., 93.
73. And, it should be noted, we can know this sort of thing without having a complete *theory* of right and wrong.
74. Kant, *Metaphysics*, 182–3.

4. Ethical Character in a Godless Universe

1. Genesis 1:26.
2. Genesis 3:16. Initially, woman is characterized by God as a "helper" and "partner" to man (Genesis 2:18). The decree that wives must obey their husbands seems to be part of the punishment for the Fall. This rule is endorsed in the New Testament by the Apostle Paul; see, for instance, Ephesians 5:22. For a defense of the view that the husband should have the final say in disagreements between husbands and wives, see Lewis, *Mere Christianity*, 104–14.
3. Genesis 3:2–5.
4. Milton, *Paradise Lost*, 222, Book IX, lines 700 and 704.
5. Ibid., 223, Book IX, line 729.
6. Ibid., 9, Book I, line 263.
7. Similarity to God is, of course, not sinful in and of itself; after all, humans are said to be made in God's image (Genesis 1:26). It is the attempt to rise above one's proper place that is sinful.
8. Lewis, *Pain* 75. Lewis, who was an atheist until his early thirties, was quite familiar with the sentiment expressed in these lines and described

God as a "transcendental interferer;" see Nicholi, Jr., *Question of God*, 46, and C. S. Lewis, *Surprised by Joy: The Shape of My Early Life* (New York: Harcourt, 1955), 172.

9. Genesis 3:19.
10. Lewis, *Pain*, 77–8.
11. Pascal, *Pensees*, #182, 53–4.
12. Plantinga, *Christian Belief*, 269.
13. Augustine, *Confessions*, trans. F. J. Sheed (Indianapolis: Hackett, 1993), 8. Interestingly, the baby's sin is envy – the very sin that lead Satan to revolt against God's rule.
14. Lewis, *Pain*, 79.
15. Ibid., 63.
16. Ibid., 78.
17. See Plantinga, *Christian Belief*, ch. 7.
18. Pascal, *Pensees*, #164, 43.
19. Jerome Neu, "Pride and Identity," in *Wicked Pleasures*, ed. R. Solomon (Lanham, MD: Rowman & Littlefield, 1999), 76.
20. 1 Corinthians 7:19.
21. Philip Quinn, "Primacy of God's Will," 284–5.
22. See Chapter 2 here.
23. Aristotle, *Ethics*, 93, NE 1123b1–5.
24. Ibid., 94, NE 1123b15–25.
25. Ibid., 95, NE 1124a1–5.
26. Ibid, 96, NE 1124b5.
27. Alasdair MacIntyre, *A Short History of Ethics*, 2nd ed. (Notre Dame: Univ. of Notre Dame Press, 1998), 79.
28. Julia Driver, *Uneasy Virtue* (Cambridge: Cambridge Univ. Press, 2001), 18.
29. Ibid., 19.
30. Aristotle, *Ethics*, 94, NE 1123b10–15.
31. C. S. Lewis, *The Screwtape Letters* (New York: Simon & Schuster, 1996), 59.
32. Ibid.
33. This point is relevant to the arguments outlined in the opening section of Chapter 5 – but I will not explore the connection here. For a relevant discussion that contains some views remarkably similar to the ones expressed by Lewis in the passages under discussion, see Russell, "Can Religion Cure Our Troubles?" in *Why I Am Not a Christian and Other Essays on Religion and Related Subjects*, ed. P. Edwards (New York: Simon & Schuster, 1957), 193–204, particularly 197.
34. Ibid. (my emphasis).
35. Aristotle, *Ethics*, 96, NE 1124a20–5.
36. If you are married, reflect on the various conditions beyond your control that had to obtain in order for that first meeting to occur, and how different your life would have been if just one of them had not obtained.

37. See Nisbett and Ross, *Human Inference*, and John Doris, *Lack of Character*.
38. Doris, ibid., 30–4.
39. Ibid., 39–53.
40. Ibid., 117.
41. 1 Corinthians 4:7.
42. Some of the points made in this discussion of naturalistic humility are similar to some points made by Saul Smilansky in "Free Will and the Mystery of Modesty," *American Philosophical Quarterly* 40:2 (April 2003), 105–17. However, Smilansky assumes the absence of libertarian free will for the sake of his discussion (see 110). For another relevant discussion, see Joseph Kupfer, "The Moral Perspective of Humility," *Pacific Philosophical Quarterly* 84 (2003), 249–69.
43. Matthew 22:39; Mark 12:31.
44. This thesis was discussed in Chapter 2.
45. For the more technically inclined, the example shows that counterfactual implication is not a transitive relation, or, alternatively, that hypothetical syllogism is not a valid rule of inference for counterfactuals. I was first exposed to this example in Ed Gettier's graduate course in modal logic taught in the spring of 1995 at UMass–Amherst.
46. According to Thomas Aquinas, charity involves not only love of one's neighbors but also love of God – see, *Treatise on the Virtues*, trans. John A. Oesterle (Notre Dame: Univ. of Notre Dame Press, 1984), 147. This corresponds to Jesus' claim that the two most important commandments are to love God and to love one's neighbors. See, for instance, Matthew 22:34–40. In Section 4.4 I am concerned just with love for one's neighbors.
47. For instance, if we introduce familial relationships into the picture, things become more complicated. I think the basic point is still correct, however.
48. Bertrand Russell, "A Free Man's Worship," in *Not a Christian*, 107.
49. Aquinas, *Virtues*, 146.
50. Bertrand Russell, "What I Believe," in *Not a Christian*, 56.
51. Ibid., 53.
52. Ibid., 54.
53. Mark Juergensmeyer, *Terror in the Mind of God* (Berkeley and Los Angeles: Univ. of California Press, 2000), 162.
54. Andrew Newberg, Eugene D'Aquili, and Vince Rause suggest that the Neanderthals had some form of religion that gave them a sense of control over the forces of nature and helped assuage their fear of death. See *Why God Won't Go Away: Brain Science and the Biology of Belief* (New York: Ballantine, 2001), 54–5. However, their views on the *origin* of religion, outlined in Chapter 7 of their book, are more complex than Russell's. One of the more outlandish theories about the origin of religious belief comes from Sigmund Freud; for a useful discussion of this view, see Nicholi, Jr., *Question*, 69–71.

55. Russell, "What I Believe," in *Not a Christian*, 55. This is the conclusion that the character of Philo reaches toward the end of Part XI of Hume's *Dialogues*, 75.
56. Russell, "A Free Man's Worship," in *Not a Christian*, 112–4 (my emphasis).
57. Lewis, *Mere Christianity*, 140–1.
58. John Kekes, *Facing Evil* (Princeton: Princeton Univ. Press, 1990), 23.
59. Ibid., 23–4. Note the similarity to Russell's remark about the "great world."
60. Ibid., 26.
61. Russell seems to recognize this third condition as well; see "What I Believe," in *Not a Christian*, 77.
62. Merrill Ring, *Beginning With the Pre-Socratics*, 2nd ed. (Mountain View, CA: Mayfield Publishing Company, 2000), 62–3; 104–18.
63. For this interpretation of Anaximander's position, see Jonathan Barnes, *The Presocratic Philosophers: Volume 1 Thales to Zeno* (London: Routledge and Kegan Paul, 1979), 23–5.
64. Plato, *Apology*, 36 (my emphasis)
65. Aristotle, *Ethics*, 22, NE 1099b20–5.
66. Gottfried Wilhelm Leibniz, *Theodicy*, trans. E. M. Huggard (La Salle, IL: Open Court, 1985), 128.
67. Leslie, *Universes*, 165–6.
68. Martin Luther King, Jr., *The Autobiography of Martin Luther King, Jr.*, ed. Clayborne Carson (New York: Warner Books, 1998), 114–5.
69. By which it is normally meant that *everything* happens for a *good* reason.
70. Steven Pinker calls this type of reasoning "the moralistic fallacy;" see *Blank Slate*, 162.
71. James Cameron, dir. *The Terminator*. Film. MGM/UA Studios (1984).
72. Kekes, *Facing Evil*, 202–5.
73. Ibid., 27.
74. Ibid., 205.
75. Ibid.
76. Ibid., 206.
77. Ibid., 207.
78. Michel de Montaigne, "That to Philosophize is to Learn to Die," trans. D. M. Frame, in *Essays* (Chicago: The Great Books Foundation, 1966), 8–9. de Montaigne attributes the idea behind the title of the essay to Cicero, but it originates with Plato; see Plato, *Phaedo*, 64a.
79. de Montaigne, "Learn to Die," 9.
80. It seems clear that the method is not foolproof; Nicholi, Jr., tells us that Freud was obsessed with his own death and reflected on it daily. However, it seemed to bring him not solace but rather the opposite; see *Question of God*, 216–30.
81. Kekes, *Facing Evil*, 211.
82. Pinker, *Blank Slate*, 265.

83. Kekes, *Facing Evil*, 186.
84. Russell, "What I Believe," in *Not a Christian*, 54.
85. Lewis, *Pain*, 88.
86. Gordon Graham, *Evil and Ethics*, 118.
87. Plato, *Meno*, trans. G. M. A. Grube (Indianapolis: Hackett, 1981), 22, 89b.
88. Plato, *Republic*, 148, 473d.
89. Even Aristotle and Hume, who think that there is in fact a significant degree of coincidence between the two, recognize the influence of contingency in this area.
90. Kekes, *Facing Evil*, 163. It should be noted that this does not imply that in the ideal state the *only* answer to the question of why one should be moral is that doing so is the best way of living. Kekes's position is consistent with the Kantian answer to the question of why one should be moral that I endorsed in Section 3.3.
91. Russell, "What I Believe," in *Not a Christian*, 81.
92. Joseph LeDoux, *The Emotional Brain* (New York: Touchstone, 1996), 135. LeDoux's book is an accessible account of the brain science of fear by a leading researcher in the field.
93. Aldous Huxley, *Brave New World* (New York: HarperCollins, 1998), 94.
94. Ibid., 41.
95. Ibid., 16.
96. Ibid., 59. The elevator operator is another counterexample to Taylor's view about what makes a life internally meaningful.
97. I think that something similar is true of another infamous literary example of moral improvement through science – the case of Alex in *A Clockwork Orange*. In the case of Alex the process itself is extremely unpleasant – but a deeper criticism of it is that it does not make Alex into a genuinely virtuous person. I develop this idea in more detail in "Pleasure, Pain, and Moral Character and Development," *Pacific Philosophical Quarterly* 83 (2002), 282–99.
98. Aristotle, *Ethics*, 31, NE 1120b25–30.
99. Kant, *Metaphysics*, 146.
100. Ibid., 223.
101. Ibid., 166.
102. Romans 7:18–9.
103. LeDoux, *Emotional Brain*, 265.
104. Antonio Damasio, *Looking for Spinoza: Joy, Sorrow, and the Feeling Brain* (Orlando, FL: Harcourt, 2003), 287–8.
105. LeDoux, *Emotional Brain*, 303.
106. Ibid.
107. Aristotle, *Ethics*, 31, NE 1120b25–30.
108. Kant, *Metaphysics*, 204.
109. The discussion that has caused much of the trouble appears in the first chapter of Kant's *Groundwork*, 65–8. For some useful discussion

of the issue, see Marcia Baron, "The Alleged Moral Repugnance of Acting From Duty," *Journal of Philosophy* 81:4 (April 1984), 197–220; Richard Henson, "What Kant Might Have Said: Moral Worth and the Overdetermination of Dutiful Action," *Philosophical Review* 88 (1979), 39–54; and Barbara Herman, "On the Value of Acting From the Motive of Duty," *Philosophical Review* 90 (1981), 359–82.

110. Kant, *Metaphysics*, 205.
111. Immanuel Kant, *Religion Within Reason*, 25.
112. Immanuel Kant, *Lectures on Ethics*, 76.
113. For a useful discussion of some other roles that the emotions might play in the psychology of a person with virtue in the Kantian sense, see Chapter 4 of Nancy Sherman's *Making a Necessity of Virtue* (Cambridge: Cambridge Univ. Press, 1997).
114. Kant, *Metaphysics*, 205.
115. Aristotle, *Ethics*, 34–5, NE 1103b20–5.
116. John Cottingham, *Meaning of Life*, 76–7.
117. Paul Kurtz, "Toward a Catholic/Humanist Dialogue," in *Secular Humanism*, 140. For a related worry, see Bill Joy, "Why the Future Doesn't Need Us," in *Taking the Red Pill: Science, Philosophy and Religion in the Matrix*, ed. G. Yeffeth (Dallas, TX: BenBella Books, 2003), 199–232.
118. For one worthwhile sliver of the controversy, see Jeffrey Record, "Bounding the Global War on Terrorism," www.carlisle.army.mil/ssi/pubs/2003/bounding/bounding.pdf (accessed March 26, 2004).
119. Flanagan, *Problem of Soul*, 311–12.
120. The point about the desire for sweet tastes is made by Robert Wright, in *The Moral Animal: Evolutionary Psychology and Everyday Life* (New York: Vintage Books, 1995), 67.
121. Russell, "The New Generation," in *Not a Christian*, 160.
122. Huxley, *Brave New World*, 228.

5. Creeds To Live By

1. Matthew 10:34.
2. Plato, *Phaedo*, 58–64, 107e–114c.
3. Ibid., 64, 114d. For similar remarks by Socrates about a different position, see *Meno*, 20, 86c.
4. Plato, *Phaedo*, 64, 114d.
5. Pascal, *Pensees*, #680, 153.
6. John Cottingham, *Meaning of Life*, 96–7.
7. Graham's argument, also discussed in Chapter 3, is in this family as well. Graham says that his argument "does not purport to prove its conclusion, but to establish reason for *presupposing* the truth of the conclusion" (see, *Evil and Ethics*, 96).
8. Exodus 9:16.
9. Exodus 19:5–6.

10. Genesis 22:1–12.
11. Exodus 23:23–7.
12. Joshua 6:20–1 (my emphasis).
13. Exodus 32:25–9.
14. Karen Armstrong, *A History of God*, 105.
15. Juergensmeyer, *Terror*, 26.
16. Armstrong, *History of God*, 197.
17. Juergensmeyer, Terror, 216.
18. Russell, "A Free Man's Worship," in *Why I Am Not a Christian*, 115.
19. Graham, *Christian Ethics*, 208.
20. Ibid.
21. Graham's argument here bears some similarity to the Kantian moral argument discussed in Chapter 3. In the preface to his book (ibid., xiii), Graham says that his argument "is essentially a version of [Kant's] so-called 'moral argument for the existence of God.'"
22. Ibid., 211.
23. Ibid.
24. Ibid., 212.
25. Ibid., 213.
26. Ibid., 214–15.
27. Although, as I said when I initially discussed the proposal in question in Chapter 4, I am *not* advocating putting the power of character-formation into the hands of the state. In fact I think this is an extremely bad idea.
28. For an extended argument that there is such a thing as human nature and that science can help us to understand it, see Pinker, *The Blank Slate*.
29. Damasio, *Looking for Spinoza*, 289.
30. Certainly much of our behavior indicates that we implicitly assume that (2) is false; for example, how many parents act as if they believe there is nothing they can do to improve the lives of their children?
31. Mill, *Utilitarianism*, 19.
32. Singer, *How?*, 235.
33. For an argument along these lines that something like this is true in the United States, see Howard Zinn, *A People's History of the United States* (New York: HarperCollins, 1999).
34. C. S. Lewis, *A Grief Observed* (New York: HarperCollins, 2001), 28.
35. Though Freud's case is not a particularly inspiring one; again, see Nicholi, Jr., *Question of God*.
36. For an account of this episode involving Hume and Boswell, see Chapter 7 of E. C. Mossner's *The Forgotten Hume* (New York: Columbia Univ. Press, 1943), 169–88.
37. For related discussions, see Robert Sapolsky, "Circling the Blanket for God," in *The Trouble with Testosterone* (New York: Touchstone, 1998), 241–88; and Paul Kurtz, "Will Humanism Replace Theism?" in *In Defense of Secular Humanism* (Amherst, NY: Prometheus Books, 1983), 190–8.

38. Newberg, D'Aquili, and Rause, *Why God Won't Go Away*, 119.
39. Ibid., 139.
40. Ibid., 172.
41. This aspect of Lewis's view may be found in Chapter 6 of *The Problem of Pain*. For an excellent literary illustration of many of the ideas put forth by Lewis in that chapter, see Leo Tolstoy's *The Death of Ivan Ilyich*, trans. L. Solotaroff (New York: Bantam Books, 1981).
42. John Stuart Mill, "Utility of Religion," in *Three Essays on Religion* (Amherst, NY: Prometheus Books, 1998), 109.
43. Ibid., 110.
44. Pascal, *Pensees*, #253, 77.
45. Lewis, *Mere Christianity*, 88.
46. Interestingly, one of the central phenomenological components of the mystical experience Unitary Absolute Being is a complete extinction of the sense of self.

REFERENCES

Adams, Robert. 1999. *Finite and infinite goods*. Oxford: Oxford Univ. Press.

Aquinas, Thomas. 1984. *Treatise on the virtues*. Trans. J. A. Oesterle. Notre Dame: Univ. of Notre Dame Press.

Aristotle. 1962. *Nicomachean ethics*. Trans. M. Ostwald. Englewood Cliffs, NJ: Prentice Hall.

Armstrong, Karen. 1993. *A history of God*. New York: Ballantine Books.

Augustine. 1993. *Confessions*. Trans. F. J. Sheed. Indianapolis: Hackett.

Aurelius, Marcus. 1805. *Meditations*. Trans. J. Collier. London: Walter Scott.

Barnes, Jonathan. 1979. *The presocratic philosophers: Volume I Thales to Zeno*. London: Routledge and Kegan Paul.

Baron, Marcia. 1984. The alleged moral repugnance of acting from duty. *Journal of Philosophy* 81: 197–220.

Behe, Michael. 1996. *Darwin's black box*. New York: Touchstone.

Blackburn, Simon. 1998. *Ruling passions*. Oxford: Oxford Univ. Press.

Boethius. 1969. *The consolation of philosophy*. Trans. V. E. Watts. New York: Penguin.

Bradley, Ben. 1998. Extrinsic value. *Philosophical Studies* 91: 109–26.

Brody, Baruch. 1974. Morality and Religion Reconsidered. In *Readings in the Philosophy of Religion*, ed. B. Brody. Englewood Cliffs, NJ: Prentice Hall.

Burgess, Anthony. 1986. *A Clockwork Orange*. New York: W.W. Norton & Company.

Cameron, James, dir. 1984. *The Terminator*. Film. MGM/UA Studios.

Camus, Albert. 1946. *The stranger*. Trans. S. Gilbert. New York: Random House.

Chisholm, Roderick. 1973. *The problem of the criterion*. Milwaukee: Marquette Univ. Press.

Conrad, Joseph. 1976. *The heart of darkness*. New York: Penguin Books.

Cottingham, John. 2003. *On the meaning of life*. New York: Routledge.

References

Craig, William Lane. 1996. "The Indispensability of Theological Meta-ethical Foundations for Morality," home.apu.edu/~CTRF/papers/1996_papers/craig.html (accessed March 26, 2004).

Craig, William Lane. 2004. "The Absurdity of Life Without God," hisdefense. org/audio/wc_audio.html (accessed March 26, 2004).

Cudworth, Ralph. 1976. *A treatise concerning eternal and immutable morality*. New York: Garland.

Damasio, Antonio. 2003. *Looking for Spinoza: Joy, sorrow, and the feeling brain*. Orlando, FL: Harcourt.

Darwall, Stephen. 1999. "Valuing Activity." In *Human Flourishing*, eds. E. F. Paul, F. D. Miller, and J. Paul. Cambridge: Cambridge Univ. Press.

Dawkins, Richard. 1996. *The blind watchmaker*. New York: W.W. Norton & Company.

Descartes, Rene. 1960. *Discourse on method and meditations*. Trans. L. J. Lafleur. New York: Macmillan.

Doris, John. 2002. *Lack of character*. Cambridge: Cambridge Univ. Press.

Dostoevsky, Fyodor. 1984. *The Brothers Karamazov*. Trans. K. Mochulski. New York: Bantam.

Draper, Paul. 1989. Pain and pleasure: An evidential problem for theists. *NOUS* 23: 331–50.

Driver, Julia. 2001. *Uneasy virtue*. Cambridge: Cambridge Univ. Press.

Edwards, Paul. 2000. "The Meaning and Value of Life." In *The Meaning of Life*, ed. E. D. Klemke, 2nd ed. Oxford: Oxford Univ. Press.

Elster, Jon. 2000. *Ulysses unbound*. Cambridge: Cambridge Univ. Press.

Epicurus. 1964. *Letters, principal doctrines, and Vatican sayings*. New York: Macmillan.

Feldman, Fred. 1992. *Confrontations with the reaper*. Oxford: Oxford Univ. Press.

Flanagan, Owen. 2002. *The problem of the soul*. New York: Basic Books.

Frank, Robert. 1988. *Passions within reason*. New York: W.W. Norton.

Graham, Gordon. 2001. *Evil and Christian ethics*. Cambridge: Cambridge Univ. Press.

Hare, John. 1996. *The moral gap*. Oxford: Clarendon Press.

———. 2001. *God's call*. Grand Rapids, MI: Wm. B. Eerdmans.

Henson, Richard. 1979. What Kant might have said: Moral worth and the overdetermination of dutiful action. *Philosophical Review* 88: 39–54.

Herman, Barbara. 1981. On the value of acting from the motive of duty. *Philosophical Review* 90: 359–82.

Hick, John. 1966. *Evil and the God of love*. New York: Macmillan.

Hume, David. 1998a. *Dialogues concerning natural religion*, 2nd ed. Indianapolis: Hackett.

————. 1998b. "Of Miracles," in *Dialogues Concerning Natural Religion*, 2ⁿᵈ ed. Indianapolis: Hackett.

————. 1998c. *An enquiry concerning the principles of morals*. Oxford: Oxford Univ. Press.

Hurka, Thomas. 1998. Two kinds of organic unity. *Journal of Ethics* 2:4: 299–320.

Huxley, Aldous. 1998. *Brave new world*. New York: HarperCollins.

Jonze, Spike. 2002. *Adaptation*. Film. Columbia Pictures.

Joy, Bill. 2003. "Why the Future Doesn't Need Us," in *Taking the Red Pill: Science, Philosophy, and Religion in the Matrix*, ed. G. Yeffeth. Dallas, TX: BenBella Books.

Juergensmeyer, Mark. 2000. *Terror in the mind of God*. Berkeley and Los Angeles: Univ. of California Press.

Kagan, Shelly. 1998. Rethinking intrinsic value. *Journal of Ethics* 2:4: 277–97.

Kant, Immanuel. 1930. *Lectures on ethics*. Trans. L. Infield. Indianapolis: Hackett.

————. 1960. *Religion within the limits of reason alone*. Trans. T. M. Greene and H. H. Hudson. New York: Harper & Row.

————. 1964. *Groundwork of the metaphysic of morals*. Trans. H. J. Paton. New York: Torchbook.

————. 1996. *The metaphysics of morals*. Trans. M. Gregor. Cambridge: Cambridge Univ. Press.

————. 1997. *Critique of practical reason*. Trans. M. Gregor. Cambridge: Cambridge Univ. Press.

Kekes, John. 1990. *Facing evil*. Princeton, NJ: Princeton Univ. Press.

King, Jr., Martin Luther. 1998. *The autobiography of Martin Luther King, Jr.*, ed. C. Carson. New York: Warner Books.

Kohn, Alfie. 1986. *No Contest: The case against competition*. Boston: Houghton Mifflin.

Kraut, Richard. 1989. *Aristotle on the human good*. Princeton, NJ: Princeton Univ. Press.

Kupfer, Joseph. 2003. The moral perspective of humility. *Pacific Philosophical Quarterly* 84: 249–69.

Kurtz, Paul. 1983a. "The Meaning of Life," in *In Defense of Secular Humanism*. Amherst, NY: Prometheus Books.

————. 1983b. "Toward a Catholic/Humanist Dialogue," in *In Defense of Secular Humanism*.

————. 1983c. "Will Humanism Replace Theism?" in *In Defense of Secular Humanism*.

LeDoux, Joseph. 1996. *The emotional brain*. New York: Touchstone.

Leibniz, Gottfried Wilhelm. 1985. *Theodicy*. Trans. E. M. Huggard. La Salle, IL: Open Court.

Leslie, John. 1989. *Universes*. New York: Routledge.

Lewis, Clive Staples. 1955. *Surprised by joy: The shape of my early life*. New York: Harcourt.

———. 1996. *The screwtape letters*. New York: Simon & Schuster.

———. 2001a. *A grief observed*. New York: HarperCollins.

———. 2001b. *Mere Christianity*. New York: HarperCollins.

———. 2001c. *Miracles*. New York: HarperCollins.

———. 2001d. *The problem of pain*. New York: HarperCollins.

MacIntyre, Alasdair. 1998. *A short history of ethics*, 2nd ed. Notre Dame: Univ. of Notre Dame Press.

Mackie, John. 1992. "Evil and Omnipotence," in *The Problem of Evil: Selected Readings*, ed. M. L. Peterson. Notre Dame: Univ. of Notre Dame Press.

Martin, Michael. 2002. *Atheism, morality, and meaning*. Amherst, NY: Prometheus Books.

Mavrodes, George. 1993. "Religion and the Queerness of Morality," in *Moral Philosophy: A Reader*, ed. L. Pojman. Indianapolis: Hackett.

Mayr, Ernst. 2001. *What evolution is*. New York: Basic Books.

Metz, Thaddeus. 2000. Could God's purpose be the source of life's meaning? *Religious Studies* 36: 293–313.

Mill, John Stuart. 1979. *Utilitarianism*. Indianapolis: Hackett.

———. 1998. "Utility of Religion," in *Three Essays on Religion*. Amherst, NY: Prometheus Books.

Miller, Christian. 2003. Social psychology and virtue ethics. *Journal of Ethics* 7: 365–92.

Milton, John. 1956. *Paradise lost*. Chicago: The Great Books Foundation.

Montaigne, de, Michel. 1966. "That To Philosophize Is To Learn To Die," in *Essays*. Trans. D.M. Frame. Chicago: The Great Books Foundation.

Moore, George Edward. 1903. *Principia ethica*. Cambridge: Cambridge Univ. Press.

Morris, Thomas. 2000. *Our idea of God*. Notre Dame: Univ. of Notre Dame Press.

Mossner, Ernest Campbell. 1943. *The forgotten Hume*. New York: Columbia Univ. Press.

Mouw, Richard. 1996. *The God who commands*. Notre Dame: Univ. of Notre Dame Press.

Murphy, Mark. 1998. Divine command, divine will, and moral obligation. *Faith and Philosophy* 15: 3–27.

Nagel, Thomas. 1979. *Mortal questions*. Cambridge: Cambridge Univ. Press.

Neu, Jerome. 1999. "Pride and Identity," in *Wicked Pleasures*, ed. R. Solomon. Lanham, MD: Rowman & Littlefield.

Newberg, Andrew., Eugene D'Aquili, and Vince Rause. 2001. *Why God won't go away: Brain science and the biology of belief.* New York: Ballantine.

Nicholi, Jr., Armand. 2002. *The question of God.* New York: Free Press.

Nielsen, Kai. 1990. *Ethics without God*, rev. ed. New York: Prometheus Books.

Nisbett, Richard E., and Lee Ross. 1980. *Human inference: Strategies and shortcomings of social judgment.* Englewood Cliffs., NJ: Prentice Hall.

Nisbett, Richard E., and Timothy D. Wilson. 1977. "Telling more than we can know: Verbal reports on mental processes." *Psychological Review* 84: 231–59.

Nozick, Robert. 1977. *Anarchy, state, and utopia.* New York: Basic Books.

Nucci, Larry. 2001. *Education in the moral domain.* Cambridge: Cambridge Univ. Press.

Pascal, Blaise. 1995. *Pensees and other writings.* Trans. H. Levi. Oxford: Oxford Univ. Press.

Pennock, Robert. 1999. *Tower of Babel.* Cambridge, MA: MIT Press.

Pinker, Steven. 2002. *The blank slate: The modern denial of human nature.* New York: Penguin Putnam.

Plantinga, Alvin. 1974. *The nature of necessity.* Oxford: Oxford Univ. Press.

———. 1998. "The Free Will Defense," in *The Analytic Theist: An Alvin Plantinga Reader*, ed. J. F. Sennett. Grand Rapids, MI: Wm. B. Eerdmans.

———. 2000. *Warranted Christian belief.* Oxford: Oxford Univ. Press.

Plato. 1948. *Euthyphro, apology, crito.* Trans. F. J. Church. New York: Macmillan.

———. 1977. *Phaedo.* Trans. G. M. A. Grube. Indianapolis: Hackett.

———. 1981. *Meno*, 2nd ed. Trans. G. M. A. Grube. Indianapolis: Hackett.

———. 1992. *Republic.* Trans. G. M. A. Grube. Indianapolis: Hackett.

———. 1993. *Philebus.* Trans. D. Frede. Indianapolis: Hackett.

———. 2000. *Timaeus.* Trans. D. J. Zeyl. Indianapolis: Hackett.

Plutarch. 1960. *The rise and fall of Athens: Nine Greek lives.* Trans. I. Scott-Kilvert. New York: Penguin Books.

Quinn, Philip. 1998. "The Primacy of God's Will in Christian Ethics," in *Christian Theism and Moral Philosophy.* Macon, GA: Mercer Univ. Press.

Ratzsch, Del. 2001. *Nature, design, and science.* New York: SUNY Press.

Record, Jeffrey. 2003. "Bounding the Global War on Terrorism." www.carlisle.army.mil/ssi/pubs/2003/bounding/bounding.pdf (accessed March 26, 2004).

Ring, Merrill. 2000. *Beginning with the Pre-Socratics*, 2nd ed. Mountain View, CA: Mayfield Publishing Company.

Russell, Bertrand. 1925. *What I believe.* New York: E. P. Dutton & Company.

———. 1957a. "A Free Man's Worship," in *Why I Am Not a Christian and Other Essays on Religion and Related Subjects*, ed. P. Edwards. New York: Simon & Schuster.

———. 1957b. "Can Religion Cure Our Troubles?" in *Why I Am Not a Christian*.

———. 1957c. "The New Generation," in *Why I Am Not a Christian*.

———. 1957d. "What I Believe," in *Why I Am Not a Christian*.

———. 1957e. "Why I Am Not a Christian," in *Why I Am Not a Christian*.

Sade, de, Marquis. 1992. *The misfortunes of virtue and other early tales*. Trans. D. Coward. Oxford: Oxford Univ. Press.

Sapolsky, Robert. 1998. "Circling the Blanket for God," in *The Trouble with Testosterone*. New York: Touchstone.

Sherman, Nancy. 1997. *Making a necessity of virtue*. Cambridge: Cambridge Univ. Press.

Shyamalan, M. Night., dir. 2002. *Signs*. Film. Touchstone Pictures.

Singer, Peter. 1995. *How are we to live? Ethics in an age of self-interest*. Amherst, NY: Prometheus Books.

Smilansky, Saul. 2003. Free will and the mystery of modesty. *American Philosophical Quarterly* 40: 105–17.

Strobel, Lee. 1998. *The case for Christ*. Grand Rapids, MI: Zondervan.

Sumption, Jonathan. 1978. *The Albigensian crusade*. London: Faber and Faber.

Swinburne, Richard. 1981. "Duty and the Will of God," in *Divine Commands and Morality*, ed. P. Helm. Oxford: Oxford Univ. Press.

Taylor, Richard. 2000. *Good and Evil*. Amherst, NY: Prometheus Books.

Tolstoy, Leo. 2000. "My Confession," in *The Meaning of Life*, ed. E. D. Klemke, 2nd ed. Oxford: Oxford Univ. Press.

Tolstoy, Leo. 1981. *The death of Ivan Ilyich*. Trans. L. Solotaroff. New York: Bantam Books.

van Inwagen, Peter. 1993. *Metaphysics*. Boulder, CO: Westview Press.

Wielenberg, Erik. 2002. Pleasure, pain, and moral character and development. *Pacific Philosophical Quarterly* 83: 282–99.

———. 2004. Egoism and *eudaimonia*-maximization in the *Nicomachean ethics*. *Oxford Studies in Ancient Philosophy* 26: 277–95.

Wierenga, Edward. 1983. "A defensible divine command theory." *NOUS* 17: 387–408.

Wolf, Susan. 2003. "The Meanings of Lives." www.law.nyu.edu/clppt/program2003/readings/wolf.pdf (accessed March 26, 2004).

Wright, Robert. 1995. *The moral animal: Evolutionary psychology and everyday life*. New York: Vintage Books.

Wurmbrand, Richard. 1967. *Tortured for Christ*. London: Hodder & Stoughton.

Zagzebski, Linda. 1990. "What If the Impossible Had Been Actual?" in *Christian Theism and the Problems of Philosophy*, ed. M. Beatty. Notre Dame: Univ. of Notre Dame Press.

Zinn, Howard. 1999. *A people's history of the United States*. New York: HarperCollins.

INDEX

189